# SPANISH COOKING

BEVERLY LEBLANC

# SPANISH COOKING

Love Food ® is an imprint of Parragon Books Ltd

Parragon
Queen Street House
4 Queen Street
Bath BA1 1HE, UK

Created and produced by The Bridgewater Book Company Ltd.
*Project Editor* Stephanie Horner
*Project Designer* Michael Whitehead
*Photography* David Jordan
*Home Economist* Judy Williams
*Additional photography* Max Alexander and Alistair Plumb

ISBN: 978-1-4075-6810-2

Printed in China

NOTES FOR THE READER

- This book uses imperial, metric, or US cup measurements. Follow the same
  units of measurement throughout; do not mix imperial and metric.

- All spoon measurements are level: teaspoons are assumed to be 5 ml, and
  tablespoons are assumed to be 15 ml.

- Unless otherwise stated, milk is assumed to be whole, eggs and individual
  vegetables such as potatoes are medium, and pepper is freshly ground
  black pepper.

- Recipes using raw or very lightly cooked eggs should be avoided by infants,
  the elderly, pregnant women, convalescents, and anyone with a chronic
  condition.

- The times given are an approximate guide only. Preparation times differ
  according to the techniques used by different people and the cooking times
  may also vary from those given.

# contents

# INTRODUCTION

# Spanish cuisine is varied and rich, reflecting and preserving generations of regional traditions.

Anyone who has visited Spain's sprawling coastal Mediterranean resorts and returned home with the impression that Spaniards only cook paella and chicken in garlic to tourist standard, will have missed out on the vast diversity of dishes eaten every day. Although at first sight home cooking might appear simple and unadorned, meals are centered round quality ingredients, with an appreciation of seasonal freshness. Hospitality and generosity also influence the Spanish appreciation of well-prepared food.

Spain's position on the Iberian Peninsula also gives it an Atlantic coastline. This simple geographical fact, along with the massive size of the country, makes it difficult to summarize Spanish cooking. The center of the country is a vast plateau with arid plains, fringed by landscapes that include Mediterranean and Atlantic coastlines and soaring mountain ranges, and the entire country can experience ferocious weather conditions ranging from searingly hot to fiercely cold. What someone from sunny Seville considers to be a "typical" meal is unlikely to be described as "typical" by a native of Pamplona.

Most Spanish food is robust and flavorsome, but the north–south culinary divide is easily recognizable: northern cooking tends to be richer than that of the south and features more meat and dairy products.

## Culinary legacies

Contemporary Spanish cooks have much to thank ancient invaders for. The Phoenicians, who arrived about 1100 BC, established a trading settlement in

*The warmth and vibrancy of Spain is reflected in its domestic architecture, as well as in its food*

what has become Cadiz, planting the first grapevines in nearby Jerez. This southwest corner of Andalusia remains Spain's sherry-producing center. Next came the Carthaginians, who made no significant culinary contributions. They were followed by the Romans, who planted the first olive trees, and thus produced the first of the now-essential oil, in about AD 210. When, in 711, the Arabian Moors conquered virtually the entire peninsula, except for Asturias and the Basque country, they expanded the groves. (Arab rule continued to 1492, when monarchs Ferdinand V and Isabella I became rulers of all Spain.)

The Moors designed and developed extensive irrigation systems, *huertas*, to support the crops they introduced to the peninsula. Both the vast irrigated farms and major cash crops survive to this day. Spanish tastes were changed forever with the successful cultivation of rice, citrus fruit, almonds, and dates, and the introduction of spices from the Middle East. Eggplants, apricots, peaches, and quinces were other Moorish imports, as well as coffee—the drink of choice for most Spanish adults today.

Homage is also paid to the Golden Age of Spanish exploration in just about every kitchen every day. There was a silver lining to Christopher Columbus' unsuccessful quest for a route to the East Indies to break the Venetian monopoly on the trade of the fabulously expensive spices—the discovery of the Caribbean islands in 1492. On his return to Spain he brought with him the bounty from the New World that was to change cooking not only in Spain, but also the whole Mediterranean. The hot and sweet peppers he introduced were instantly included in cooking, their use first spreading by word of mouth through the extensive network of monasteries.

Columbus also introduced tobacco, exotic new fruit, and vegetables such as yams and sweet potatoes. On his third voyage in 1502, he captured a Mayan trading boat laden with the cocoa beans that were used as a trading currency. Ferdinand was unimpressed by the new commodity, and not until after 1528, when Hernán Cortés returned to Spain with the Aztec chocolate-making equipment, did chocolate become the rage at court and eventually all over Spain. The first commercial shipment of cocoa beans arrived in 1585; the trade has never ceased. The love affair continues, with *chocolaterías* in all towns and cities today. Columbus didn't live long enough to see his discovery become a hot drink, but for many Spaniards the traditional breakfast consists of deep-fried strips of choux pastry called *churros*, served with a glass of hot chocolate almost too thick to drink.

Although dishes with traditional Moorish influences abound, especially in restaurants, and cosmopolitan Spaniards still eat many dishes their grandparents enjoyed, Spanish cooking isn't preserved in aspic. Today, food processors and blenders are more likely to

## *Barcelona's La Boqueria market...has been trading since the 18th century*

have been, with vendors selling shimmering seafood of all kinds, freshly butchered meat carcasses, preserved meat products, and the most luscious-looking fruit and vegetables. Even in major cities, where more and more women work out of the home, market shopping flourishes. Barcelona's La Boqueria market, on Las Ramblas, the social heart of the city, for example, has been trading since the 18th century, and is one of the greatest in Europe. It is open throughout the day, but trade really picks up early evening as locals shop on their way home. (The small, café-style restaurants in the market cook meat and seafood to order, providing an inexpensive lunch stop —and the food could not be fresher.) And, bustling and vibrant as La Boqueria is, it is only one of several markets in the city, all thriving. Fusion cooking, the pairing of cuisines from different sides of the globe that is evident in other European countries, has had little influence here. Chinese restaurants do thrive in some large cities, but their flavorings, cooking techniques, and ingredients are not incorporated in mainstream Spanish cooking.

## Eating the Spanish way

It has been said that Spaniards eat all day and part of the night. Most urban workers start with a light breakfast and continue to eat and snack all day until they finally sit down to an evening meal, which can be as late as 10 pm. (For schoolchildren, the evening meal is *merienda*, served about 6 pm.)

The Spanish work day starts with *el desayuno*, a quick, light breakfast of coffee with a pastry, either at home or in a café or bar on the way to work. Coffee bars always offer a supply of fresh croissants and bread rolls, and in Madrid *churros con chocolate* are

Above *Storks return to their nests each year, flying in, like tourists, from foreign climes*

Overleaf *Painted houses form a colorful backdrop on the bank of the river in Girona, in Catalonia*

be used than mortars and pestles, and modern kitchens feature all the latest appliances.

Spanish supermarkets are large and busy, and, of course, fast-food restaurants are springing up, but the tradition of daily market shopping for fresh fruit, vegetables, and seafood continues. Market days in rural communities are as important as they always

*Tapas bars open at about 1 pm, offering their array of delicacies, which are enjoyed before* la comida, *the main meal of the day*

a traditional treat that were once sold from vendors on every street corner. Today, these long, thin deep-fried fritters, dusted with sugar and cinnamon, are served with a cup of rich, dark Spanish hot chocolate at *churrerías* and cafés. For office workers, by 10 or 10.30 am it is time for an espresso and perhaps a slice of cake or a pastry, just to take the edge off their hunger. Or they might stop round 11 am for *las onces* (elevenses), or for *almuerzo* (lunch), depending on when they prefer their main meal. Tapas bars open at about 1 pm, offering their array of delicacies (see page 35), which are enjoyed before *la comida*, the

main meal of the day for many people. Offices generally close at 1.30 or 2 pm for several hours to allow employees to return home, where two or three small courses and a bottle of wine will be waiting. *La comida* for a working professional, for example, may consist of pasta or rice followed by sausages or steak or a fish dish, then fruit or yogurt. Sausages with Lentils (see page 147) is a typical *comida* dish, as are simplified versions of *cocidos*, which are Spanish hotchpotches (see page 32). Then it's back to work for a couple of hours. Afterward many Spaniards will stop for a drink and tapas with colleagues on the way home. *La cena*, the evening meal, at home might be lighter than *la comida*, consisting of soup or omelet, followed by cheese or fruit. It will be eaten at about 8.30 pm in winter and more like 9.30 pm in summer. If dinner is at a restaurant, the booking will be about 10 pm for a leisurely three-course meal, finishing round midnight. After a good night's sleep it will be time for the following day's *desayuno*.

Above *The sinuous curves of Gaudí's work in the Park Guel in Barcelona*

Left *Imposing arches on a grand scale make a dramatic setting for dining alfresco*

*Andalusia is home to many of the dishes foreigners think of as quintessentially Spanish*

## The Spanish regions

For the traveler through Spain, the cuisine varies with the scenery. Each region offers local specialties, treating similar ingredients differently to produce distinctive flavors. Tortilla, the humble thick, flat egg-and-potato omelet, is one of the few dishes usually available everywhere, but even that is prepared with regional variations (see page 42). Not surprisingly, the natural partners for regional dishes are the local wines.

### Andalusia

This is the land of flamenco dancing, bullfights, and beautiful, elegant Moorish architecture. A traditional dish in Córdoba, in the heart of ancient Arab Spain, is *rabo de toro*, or bulltail stew. Elsewhere, the region's cuisine showcases the Moorish legacy in Spanish cooking with the abundant use of spices and dried and fresh fruit. Andalusia is home to many of the dishes foreigners think of as quintessentially Spanish. Chilled tomato-and-bell-pepper Gazpacho (see page 99), for example, is one of the best-known soups in the world, and a pitcher of chilled Sangria (see page 253), the red wine and fruit punch, immediately evokes images of sunny Spain. The azure-blue Mediterranean waters supply constant seafood, and the semiarid land supports fruit-laden vineyards and olive groves. The picturesque *bodegas* of Jerez produce the finest sherries in the world.

The heat and long hours of sunshine mean there is an abundance of large sweet peppers, juicy tomatoes, oil-rich olives, and citrus fruit, as well as a dazzling array of fruit that northern Europeans consider exotic, but which are commonplace here—figs, pomegranates, persimmons, and passion fruit. A dish described as *a la andaluza* will contain a colorful, thirst-quenching mixture of sweet peppers, tomatoes, and possibly fruit. Seville oranges, so favored by the British to make marmalade, are only grown round Seville, and the use of their bitter juice appears in recipes from the Middle Ages.

The variety of tapas served in Seville's restaurants and bars is renowned. The deep-fried dishes, such as Deep-Fried Seafood (see page 159), are especially good—no one who drives along the Costa del Sol coast road will be disappointed at even the most humble seaside restaurant with a plate of pan-fried squid rings (*calamares*). It's not for nothing that Andalusia is known as the "skillet of Spain," or the *zona de los fritos*—the region of pan-fried foods.

Inland, the terrain is more rugged, with breathtaking mountain roads that eventually reach Spain's highest peaks, the snow-capped Sierra Nevada. Here, in villages such as Jabugo and Trevélez, you find the cured air-dried mountain ham, *jamón serrano* (see page 32), prized the world over for its tender, salty meat. It can flavor cooked dishes, such as Paprika Chicken on a Bed of Onions and Ham (see page 131), but to appreciate its character, nibble unadorned slices while sipping *fino* sherry before a meal.

### Aragon

Medieval hilltop towns with rough stone houses dot this ancient kingdom that nestles along the Pyrenees. Here, Arab and Christian cultures thrived together. The region is landlocked, with a varying and harsh climate—summers can be scorching, while winter will be freezing, with heavy snowfalls.

*Every coastal village has its fishing harbor. Tiny boats bring in the daily catch for the markets and restaurants*

# The fertile central basin along the Ebro River, near Zaragoza, yields vegetables, fruit, and almonds, and...flavorsome oil

Such extremes mean simple, hearty fare is the order of the day, although the Arab influence is evident in the spiced fruit desserts.

For hundreds of years, shepherds have tended the long-haired Lacha sheep that graze in the foothills and provide delicious meat and cheeses. The tradition of nomadic herders means Aragon has a culinary history of preserved foods, including air-dried hams and dried salt cod, that are easily transported without spoiling. This region also enjoys other good pork products, such as blood sausage (*morcilla*), used to flavor a traditional lamb and white bean stew. Or the blood sausage is cooked in the hard cider drunk here, in dishes similar to those from Normandy in northern France. Numerous rivers give rise to many recipes in which trout features.

Robust *chilindrón* stews, made with lamb, chicken, or pork, such as Pork with Bell Peppers (see page 140), have always been eaten here. These warming dishes are flavored by the generous use of sweet bell peppers and dried, hot chile peppers.

The fertile central basin along the Ebro River, near Zaragoza, yields vegetables, fruit, and almonds, and the olive groves produce flavorsome oil. Vegetables and oil are married in *menestra*, a slowly cooked stew that is the feature of summer meals here. Cariñena is known for its full-bodied, deeply colored red wines.

## Balearic Islands
"Floating" in the Mediterranean, the Balearic archipelago (Majorca, Minorca, Ibiza, Formentera,

*Spain is a predominantly Catholic country and boasts some extravagantly detailed church architecture*

and Cabrera) gets most of its culinary influences from mainland Catalonia, yet the islands' food has distinctive characteristics. For visitors, however, it's necessary to travel away from the pulsating coastal tourist centers to sample traditional fare.

Islanders enjoy simply prepared food, making the most of lush vegetables and copious Mediterranean seafood, especially spiny lobsters, which are eaten by the plateful all summer long. Pork often features in meals and pork fat is used for cooking. *Sobrasada*, Majorca's sweet and peppery pork sausage, is popular all over Spain for its soft, spreadable texture, as well as its spicy flavor.

Traditional one-pot meals and hearty soups provide substance for agricultural workers and seafarers. A *sopa mallorquina*, for example, is so packed with vegetables and pork the soup is almost secondary. *Coca mallorquina* is Majorca's answer to the Italian pizza. *Coques* (the plural of *coca*), which are also enjoyed on the other islands, are easy to make at home (see page 68), and the topping can be anything from leftovers to canned seafood or vegetables.

Grapes have been grown and wine has been produced on Majorca since Roman times, but little is exported. During the 18th-century British occupation, Minorca's wild juniper berries were put to use in gin production, which continues to this day.

Although the French always dispute this culinary legend, Spanish food historians claim mayonnaise had its origins here, rather than in France, and was eaten by the Duc de Richelieu first in Máhon, the capital of Minorca. As the legend continues, he then took the creamy egg emulsion to Paris, calling it *sauce mahonnaise*. (The fact that Catalans were

*The appreciation of good food and cooking is more than just a pleasant pastime in this fiercely independent part of Spain*

already making a garlic and oil emulsion that eventually had eggs incorporated to make a creamy sauce (see page 232) gives a certain amount of credibility to this version of food history.)

Minorca also produces one of the stars of Spanish cheese-making: Máhon, a pasteurized cow's milk cheese with a creamy, soft texture that hardens with age.

## Basque country

The appreciation of good food and cooking is more than just a pleasant pastime in this fiercely independent part of Spain—it is said the Basques live to eat, rather than eat to live. It is also estimated there is one restaurant for every 1,000 inhabitants here, and there isn't any question of the kitchen being solely the woman's domain. All-male gastronomic societies have been established for longer than a century. The Basques are universally recognized as excellent cooks.

As in the neighboring French Basque region, Spanish Basques cook with generous amounts of butter and cream. This, along with their own language, customs, and traditions, sets them apart from other Spaniards. Try Basque Scrambled Eggs (see page 106) for an example of how local cooks handle the popular Spanish eggs, or Pan-Fried Milk (see page 222) for a rich dessert. It was here that the French style of *nouvelle cuisine* made its first inroad into Spain in the form of *nueva cocina vasca*.

The Basque love of eating is well supplied by the fresh vegetables of neighboring Navarre, with game and exotic mushrooms from the Pyrenees, seafood from the Bay of Biscay, and the full-bodied wines from Navarre and La Rioja. Dishes from the region are easily identified when *a la vizcaína* appears in the title, indicating it contains onions and peppers, often specifically the chile pepper *choricero*.

The Basques have been fishermen for generations, so the Bay of Biscay's fish and shellfish frequently appear on the table. Hake is popular, along with baby eels, spider crabs, oysters, mussels, and tuna. *Bacalao* (dried salt cod) remains a favorite ingredient, a reminder of the days when the fresh catch had to be dried on board fishing vessels far from home. The simple tomato and sweet pepper dish *bacalao a la vizcaína* is one example of the local treatment. Basques take great pleasure in serving visitors a bowl of *angulas*, tiny, thin baby eels that look as if they are swimming in soup.

This is also the part of the country where beef can take center-stage, as many consider it the best in the country. Tapas are also a firm part of Basque culture. A full evening meal is often replaced by a couple of hours in a tapas bar, enjoying the varied selection of tidbits—notoriously larger here than in other parts of Spain.

## Canary Islands

These sun-drenched volcanic islands in the Atlantic Ocean—Grand Canary, Tenerife, Lanzarote, La Palma, Gomera, Hierro, and Fuerteventura—are closer to Africa than the Iberian peninsula and enjoy a semi-tropical climate. As Spanish and Portuguese explorers set out in search of foreign riches during the 15th century, the Canary Islands, annexed to Spain in 1496, became an important staging post before ships set off to make, or returned from, long journeys.

Fresh produce abounds, especially large tomatoes and bananas that are exported throughout Europe.

*Olive trees positively thrive in the seemingly barren wastes and searing sun of the Spanish interior*

fill up agricultural workers before a day's labors, or the mixture was used to thicken soups and stews. Fresh mackerel, tuna, and sardines feature in meals here, often served simply broiled with olive oil and garlic, or combined in a stew.

Sugar cane, originally introduced in the 16th century, thrives in the volcanic ash, and is made into rum, giving the islands an almost Caribbean feel.

## Castilla-La Mancha & Madrid

The vast arid plateau of Castile-La Mancha in central Spain is where Cervantes' fictional Don Quixote tilted at the windmills that dot this landscape. The name La Mancha comes from the Arab word *manxa*, which means dry, and it accurately describes the sun-baked, unirrigated land—in summer the sun is unrelenting. Yet some of Spain's finest ingredients grow here: the expensive saffron (see page 33), grapes, olives, and sunflowers all thrive.

Driving south from Madrid the harshness is evident as you pass through one sparsely populated dusty village after another. Food is simple, meant to provide subsistence and strength for hard laboring on the land. You will find lamb dishes and game in season. *Ollas* are meat and bean stews that provide a filling meal in a pot (see page 32). Served since the 16th century, the legendary hero Don Quixote dined on an *olla* that consisted of "more beef than mutton."

In a poor region like this, eggs have always featured. Hens were never expensive to keep, and the logic was that if you fed the hen, it would feed you. Tortilla (see page 42) and Eggs on Vegetables (see page 177) are examples of the inexpensive dishes from La Mancha. Vegetables are slowly stewed in *pisto manchego*, not unlike the French ratatouille. *Gazpacho manchego*, the regional bread-thickened

Favorite local dishes include *empañadas*, meat-and-vegetable pasty-like pies that make excellent snacks as well as simple meals. *Papas arraguadas*, "Wrinkled" Potatoes (see page 84), are served with one of the vinegar and sweet pepper *mojo* sauces. The dish gets its name from the potatoes' wrinkled appearance after being boiled in salty water. *Mojo Rojo*, red Mojo Sauce (see page 84), is one of the traditional sauces; there is also a green, cilantro-flavored version, *Mojo Verde*. A dish with an ancient heritage is *gofio*, or poor man's bread, made from toasted and ground wheat, barley, cornmeal, and sometimes chickpea flours. Baked into an unleavened bread, it served to

soup, provides warmth against the harsh winds that sweep across the plains, and is likely to contain whatever is available to go into the pot, be it meat or vegetables—very different indeed from the chilled gazpacho of Andalusia.

Ancient Toledo, with its crowded winding streets, is the home of Spanish marzipan (see page 225), which was "invented" by Moorish bakers in the 13th century. Today, numerous stores sell small Nativity figures molded out of marzipan, which are eaten all over Spain in the run-up to Christmas.

The sleepy town of Consuegra, the center of the saffron industry (see page 33), shakes off its usual dusty appearance at the end of October with the annual Fiesta de la Rosa del Azafrán, or saffron festival, when the saffron harvest is finished.

La Mancha also contains Spain's largest wine region, with the best wine produced round Valdepeñas. Most of the region's production, however, is *vino comun*, or table wine for everyday drinking.

In cosmopolitan Madrid, though, food is more lavish and lighter, reflecting the capital's historical links with royal courts. Leisurely meals are as much about enjoyment as simply fueling the body, and the numerous tapas bars round the Plaza Mayor provide pleasant meeting places for *madrileños* and tourists alike.

For a taste of traditional Madrid cuisine, try *cocido madrileño* (Madrid hotchpotch), a one-pot feast served over three courses. The meal starts with the richly flavored soup containing cooked rice. Next, the vegetables of the dish—cabbage, carrots, potatoes, and tender chickpeas—are presented. Finally, it is time for the selection of meats that have been simmered until meltingly tender. A typical combination might be beef, chorizo sausage, pork

*Spain's vast, arid central plateau, with its famous windmills, is the home of simply cooked meat and bean dishes*

## La Mancha also contains Spain's largest wine region, with the best wine produced round Valdepeñas

shoulder, chicken, and tiny meatballs. Little wonder that the three courses are referred to as the *sato, caballo,* and *rey,* or jack, queen, and king, as the dish is said to increase in nobility as the meal progresses.

### Castilla y Leon and La Rioja
Gastronomically, these regions are linked because of strong historical and geographical ties. This is the land of *asados,* or roasted meats. For many, the best, tenderest meat in Spain comes from here, especially round Segovia, where the most desirable are the *cochinillo* (suckling pig) and *lechazo* (milk-fed baby lamb), which have been roasted here since the 15th century. They are butchered at around three weeks, and the cooked meat is said to be so tender it can be cut with the edge of a plate. The conical adobe ovens traditionally used to spit-roast these delicacies over burning vine clippings (*hornos de asar*) were found originally in bakeries, as most farmhouse ovens— where they even existed—were too small to roast whole animals.

Spaniards almost always eat bread with meals, but here a meal simply isn't considered complete if bread isn't served. For centuries pilgrims bound for Santiago de Compostela have stopped in Astogra to relish the rolls (*mantecades*) said to "bulk large in the hand and light on the stomach." Perfect partners for the bread are the simple bean and vegetable stews that were once the mainstay of daily diets. *Sopa de ajo,* or garlic soup, once a peasant soup of garlic, eggs, and bread, now appears on restaurant menus everywhere.

The Andalusian custom of preserving foods *en escabeche,* in vinegar, was embraced and perfected

*Cooks in other parts of Spain must look with envy at the riches from the Mediterranean and Pyrenees that Catalan cooks choose from*

here, and everything from vegetables to game gets the treatment. You can experience the fresh taste of this preserving style with Pickled Mackerel (see page 53) or Veal with Pickled Vegetables (see page 139).

Ribera del Duero, the wine region of Castilla y Léon located along the Duero River that winds its way from Portugal to Madrid, produces predominantly fine red wines. Fertile soils and mountainous terrain combine to make La Rioja, which takes its name from the Oja River (Río Oja), the home of the full-bodied red and white Rioja wines, some of the finest in Spain. Wines have been produced here since Roman times, but were undistinguished until the late 19th century when phylloxera wiped out the French vines, and Bordeaux winemakers moved to the region.

Surprisingly, wines do not often feature much in cooking, except the popular dessert of fruit poached in wine. A recipe with *a la riojana* in the title does not mean that the dish includes wine, rather that sweet peppers are an important ingredient, because this is the center of Spain's sweet pepper-growing farms. (The sweet peppers Spanish cooks use will always be the long, pointed ones, which are much sweeter and more flavorsome than the bell-shaped peppers produced under glass in northern Europe. Look out for this pointed variety, described as Mediterranean-style peppers, in most supermarkets.) The full-bodied and simple food from here often includes beans and sweet peppers, such as in Lamb Stew with Chickpeas (see page 144). Asparagus and cardoons are grown in La Rioja too, and *menesta*

*riojana* is a simmered stew of vegetables. A typical flavoring of the Riojan dishes here comes from the combination of fruit, garlic, olive oil, onions, nuts, and tomatoes that grow throughout the region.

## Catalonia

Barcelona, Spain's largest city and the capital of this independently minded region, is considered by many also to be Spain's gastronomic capital. Stay away from harborside tourist restaurants and you will eat and drink well here for less than in most other major European cities. Catalan cuisine is not fancy or heavily sauced, instead relying on the flavors of fresh, seasonal ingredients. It is an ancient cuisine, with Can Culleretes restaurant, supposedly the oldest in Barcelona, dating from 1786. And a Catalan is credited with writing the oldest published Spanish cookbook—in the early 1500s.

Catalan cooking is distinguished by four classic sauces that provide the backbone of most cooked dishes. *Sofregit* is slow-cooked onions and tomatoes, and sometimes garlic, used at the start of cooking; *picada* is a mixture of cooked bread, garlic, olive oil, and nuts pounded with a pestle in a mortar used to thicken and flavor many dishes; *samfaina* is the all-purpose Catalan version of ratatouille that is just as often stirred into stews as a flavoring as served on its own as a vegetable dish; *Allioli* (see page 232) is a garlic-flavored mayonnaise that is served with everything from pan-fried potatoes to seafood stews. Some food writers argue that Romesco Sauce (see page 233), a mixture of toasted nuts, the dried local *romesco* chile, and tomatoes, which accompanies local seafood dishes, should be added to the list.

Cooks in other parts of Spain must look with envy at the riches from the Mediterranean and Pyrenees that Catalan cooks choose from. Their ingredients range from Alpine-like mushrooms to the freshest just-caught crustaceans, and plenty of cereals,

*Barcelona and its port. The tree-lined avenue is Las Ramblas, meaning the walkway*

page 169), which comprises pieces of cod served on tender young spinach flavored with raisins and pine nuts, reflects the Arab style of using dried fruit in savory recipes. *Fidenà*, a seafood casserole with thin pieces of pasta called *fidens*, is a popular restaurant dish, but difficult to master at home. *Romesco de pescado* is one of the many versions of seafood stew, this one made with white beans and flavored by a good spoonful of Romesco Sauce (see page 233) as it finishes cooking.

Yet, even with all the fresh ingredients on offer, Catalan cooks are masters at preparing *bacalao* (dried salt cod). A quintessential Catalan speciality is *Esqueixada*, a raw salt cod salad lightly dressed with extra virgin olive oil and vinegar and garnished with finely diced tomatoes (see page 89).

Broiling and barbecuing are popular methods of cooking, ideal for both meat and seafood. The arrival of spring is heralded with broiled *calçots* (scallions) for dipping in Romesco Sauce.

## Cantabria

The Bay of Biscay offers an abundance of fresh tuna, bonito, sardines, and anchovies to the cooks of this small region along the Costa Verde (Green Coast), while inland waters supply salmon and trout.

Santander is a holiday destination for many Spaniards and northern Europeans and the entire region is dotted with simple, family-run seafood restaurants. You'll also find plenty of broiled meats on the menu. Orchards provide the apples that are used in sweet tarts and local cakes.

A large dairy industry here means milk is used extensively in cooking, and the rich desserts include Pan-Fried Milk (see page 222) and creamy rice puddings, such as *Arroz con Leche* (see page 196).

vegetables, fruit, olives and oil, pork, and game. (Pork fat replaces olive oil in traditional Catalan recipes.) And, of course, as Barcelona is one of the Mediterranean's major ports, produce and goods from other countries enter Spain here, increasing what is on offer. One look at the covered La Boqueria market illustrates just what an international cornucopia Catalans enjoy.

The supply of fresh Mediterranean fish is varied and abundant. Black Rice (see page 122) is a regional speciality of squid and rice, flavored and colored with the squid's black ink. Cod with Spinach (see

## Extremadura

Village life can seem almost timeless in this sparsely populated "extreme and hard" land, bordering Portugal. The mountain farms produce some of Spain's most gastronomically valued pork products. Black Iberian pigs graze on nuts and acorns from the stone oak and cork trees, which are said to flavor the leg meat that is salt cured and dried, when it becomes the delicious *jamón iberico* (see page 32). The meat is cured in salt then left to mature in cellars for up to two years. Some of the finest comes from Montánchez.

Nothing is wasted, and the remainder of the pig is combined with the locally produced paprika to make what some consider to be the best chorizo in Spain.

*Relaxed social events, such as this alfresco performance, are very much part of the Spanish way of life*

Paprika production is big here, and *pimentón de la Vera* is the *denominación de origen* that guarantees its quality.

## Galicia

The Moorish culinary influence is less evident in Galicia than other parts of Spain, and the light Mediterranean cooking might as well be from a different country.

Nestled in Spain's northwest corner, Galicia takes a battering from the fierce Atlantic winds. It has the longest coastline of any Spanish region, with Europe's largest port at Vigo, so shellfish and seafood are common ingredients in its distinctive cuisine. The local clams, oysters, and scallops are renowned, and Atlantic fish such as flounder, mackerel, and sea bass are also popular. The local northern version of the more famous Mediterranean fish stew, *bouillabaisse*, is *caldereta de pescado*.

The scallop shell, symbol of St James the Apostle, is carried by pilgrims who arrive at the cathedral town of Santiago de Compostela, as they have since the Middle Ages. St James is the patron saint of Spain, so the National Day celebrations in this medieval town on 25 July are lively and elaborate. There is plenty to eat throughout the day, culminating with a slice of the local Almond Tart (see page 218).

Lush, green pastures mean meat, especially pork and game, is enjoyed here. As in Portugal, shellfish and meat are combined in simmered casseroles, such as clams with pork. Galician cooks also use butter and shortening to add a richness to cooking that is not evident in the regions that use olive oil.

*Pimientos de Padrón*, the tiny green sweet peppers that Spaniards munch deep-fried (see page 37), are grown here. Tetilla, a breast-shaped cow's milk cheese, also comes from Galicia.

The dry white wines produced in Galicia's vineyards make perfect partners for the shellfish recipes, and the bone-dry reds are ideal to complement the rich meat dishes of the region.

## The Levant

This fertile region, along the Mediterranean, which comprises the provinces of Valencia, Alicante, and Murcia between Andalusia and Catalonia, grows the fruit and vegetables the rest of Spain and much of Europe enjoy. Valencia is rice country. Rice paddies round Lake Albufera, south of the city of Valencia, produce the tons of short-grain rice that feed most of the country. Calasparra rice, from Murcia,

# *Paella...is unbeatable for adding a Spanish flavor when you are feeding a crowd*

considered by many the finest, is grown on terraces that were built by the Moors in the 12th century.

*La paella* is the best-known dish of the region, with references to it in travelers' journals from the 14th century. This classic rice dish, traditionally cooked outdoors as a meatless Lenten meal, gets its name from the shallow two-handled pan it is cooked in, a *paella*, which comes from the Latin word for a "pan." Visit any Spanish market and you will find paella pans on sale that range in size from 12 inches to several yards wide, large enough to feed an entire village. Paella pans, with their sloping sides, are specifically designed to expose a wide surface area so the liquid evaporates before the rice becomes overcooked, and to ensure even heat distribution over a fire. They are available from cookware stores, but you can also use a flameproof earthenware or cast-iron casserole, or a large, shallow skillet with an ovenproof handle.

Paella is adaptable to whatever ingredients are available, whether seafood, meat, poultry, or vegetables. The dish is unbeatable for adding a Spanish flavor when you are feeding a crowd, but it takes time and attention to make a good paella. (If you want a quick alternative, try the Rice with Chorizo and Shrimp recipe on page 125.)

Another rice speciality, *all-i-pebre*, or garlic and sweet peppers, gives no hint of its main ingredient of eels. Fisherman once prepared *arroz a banda*, or rice and seafood, to eat on board fishing vessels, but now it seems as if every restaurant along the coast prepares this saffron- and fish stock-flavored dish, which is eaten in two courses—rice first and then the

## The elegant palm groves of Elche are unique in Europe

fish with Garlic Mayonnaise (see page 232). The vast salt marshes in the region give rise to fish dishes baked in salt, which creates a thick "container" to seal in all moisture and freshness. During baking the coating becomes so solid the salt casing has to be broken with a mallet at the table.

The combination of rice and beans in *moros y cristianos*, or Moors and Christians (see page 182), is a legacy from ancient wars when the region was controlled by Arabs before El Cid won it back for the Christians.

Valencia is also where oranges reign supreme, and find their way into many savory and sweet dishes; most of the country's lemons are grown here, too. Valencia oranges are one of Spain's major export items. The combination of potatoes and orange is recognized as *a la valenciana*, and the tradition of cooking seafood in orange juice goes back to the Middle Ages. Try the Orange and Fennel Salad (see page 109) for a taste of the region.

Milk is extracted from a tiny tuber that grows here called the *chufa*, or tiger nut, to make a mild-tasting drink called *horchata*.

Murcia is the land of juicy red tomatoes, large globe artichokes, other tender green vegetables, and succulent fruit, all grown in the semiarid land away from the coast with the extensive irrigation systems developed by the Moors. This is where you'll find colorful salads utilizing the variety of produce, such as Broiled Bell Pepper Salad (see page 178) and Tuna and Bean Salad (see page 181). The tiny capers that add a rich flavor to so many Mediterranean dishes grow here, too, for packing in salt or oil. On the back of such extensive agriculture, the region is also one of the major centers of Spain's vegetable canning

industry—one look at the supermarket shelves confirms what a significant industry this is.

The elegant palm groves of Elche are unique in Europe, and provide the main ingredient for sweetmeats, such as Dates Stuffed with Spanish Marzipan (see page 225).

Traditional seafood recipes have always featured along this sunny Mediterranean coast, with hake, tuna, gray mullet, and giant shrimp plentiful. Yet, even with so much fresh seafood, salt-cured blue-fin tuna (*mojama*) is a local specialty.

### Navarre

Southern Navarre nestles between La Rioja and Aragón, so chile pepper-flavored lamb *chilindróns* are popular here, flavored with the *del choriceros* or *del pico* chile peppers that flourish on the banks of the Ebro River. Lamb and pork are the meats of choice, as the beef is often destined for the bullring, rather than tables. At the daring running of the bulls each July in Pamplona, *pastel de conejo*, a rabbit pie, is a regular feature of evening meals.

The white asparagus that is grown here is eaten throughout Spain as a spring delicacy. Humble *migas*, pan-fried bread cubes, have made their way from peasant mountain cooking to tapas bars everywhere, but here they are also served with chocolate sauce or grapes. Another regional use of chocolate is to cook game birds in a dark chocolate sauce.

Restaurant menus often feature *truchas a la navarra*, river trout marinated in the local robust red wines with herbs and spices, and then poached in the marinade. Mountain shepherds, though, simply cook their freshly caught trout in pans over open fires of wild herb cuttings, adding diced *serrano* ham for extra flavoring.

*Hotels and apartment blocks hug Spain's beaches to accommodate the influx of tourists and holidaymakers*

# In the Spanish kitchen

**Almonds (almendras)** These rich, creamy nuts feature in almost every aspect of Spanish cooking, savory and sweet. The Moors introduced almonds trees, planting the first groves near Granada in Andalusia. At their simplest, a plate of almonds is a tapas. Ground almonds are used as a thickening agent or as a replacement for some flour in desserts, but their starring role in Spanish cuisine is in candies, especially **turrón**. Almonds quickly become rancid because of their high fat content: store them in a cool, dark place, the fridge—even the freezer. Buy unblanched almonds as the skins help prevent the nuts drying out (see page 50 for how to blanch almonds.)

**Cheese (queso)** *Manchego*, a renowned sheep's milk cheese from La Mancha, is believed by many foreigners to be Spain's only cheese, but the choice is vast, with traditional cheeses made from cow's, sheep's, and goat milks, or from a mixture of milks. Some food writers claim Spain has more individual cheeses than neighboring France, although many are regional and not exported, or even available in other parts of the country.

**Chickpeas (garbanzos)** Spanish explorers introduced these slightly nutty, rich, round legumes from the New World. In their dried form they need overnight soaking and boiling before they become tender and edible, but Spanish cooks save time by buying them in cans or on market stalls *en remojo*—soaked and ready for cooking.

**Chile peppers (pimientos chili)** Heat in a Spanish dish will most likely be provided by red chile peppers, but their use is more judicious than is often assumed. The robust mountain dishes from the northwest are flavored with tiny *guindilla* peppers—these are hottest of all. The sweet, but still with heat, *romesco* peppers are used in Catalonia's Romesco Sauce, but as these are not widely available, *ñora* (or *nyora*), peppers are a good substitute.

The *choricero* chile provides the flavor and distinctive red-orange color of chorizo sausages.

**Chorizo sausage (chorizo)** Spain has a wonderful and varied selection of cured and raw sausages, of which one of the best known is chorizo. All chorizos are made from pork and contain paprika made from the *choricero* chile pepper, but beyond that the variety seems endless. Chorizos can be thick, thin, smoked, unsmoked, mildly flavored or spicy, and contain varying amounts of fat.

**Garlic (ajo)** Desserts are probably the only Spanish dishes that do not include this pungent vegetable. The bleak, dusty plains of La Mancha are home to Spain's garlic-growing industry. Buy firm, plump heads with a tight white outer skin, and store in a cool, dry place. The bulb should remain fresh for a month, but once a head has been broken into, the individual cloves will start to dry out and should be used within 10 days.

**Ham (jamón)** In a country where the pig is king, hams have been produced for at least 2,000 years. *Serrano* ham is a generic term for the salt-cured, breeze-dried leg meat of pigs from mountainous regions. The most prized hams are those made from black Iberian pigs, especially round Jabugo, Lèrida, Montánchez, Teruel, and Trevélez. A long maturation period is one reason the best ham is expensive; the other is that it is often hand-sliced. Less expensive ham is used in cooking, but the finest is served raw as a tapas. Italian prosciutto is an acceptable substitute. Cooked ham is *jamón cocido*.

**Hotchpotch stews (cocidos)** These are stews that feature in most regions, the ultimate being *cocido madrileño*, an enormous feast of three courses (see page 25). *Olla*, meaning "pot," is another name for these one-pot meals.

**Olive oil (aceite de oliva)** This is the most important ingredient in the Spanish kitchen. It is used in all types of cooking, as a flavoring and as a preservative, even as the main source of fat in many baking recipes, where other cuisines use animal fats. Spain is the largest olive oil producer in the world. Strict labeling regulations cover the olive oil grades, which are determined by the process used to extract the oil and the amount of oleic acid. Extra virgin (*aceite de oliva virgen extra*) is the finest quality from the first cold pressing. Virgin (*aceite de oliva virgen*) is also cold pressed, but not as refined as extra virgin. Oil simply labeled "olive oil" (*aceite de oliva*) is a blend of virgin and refined olive oils. It is exported, but more difficult to find than the extra virgin. There is little point in using the finest extra virgin oils for cooking, as the subtle flavors are destroyed by intense heat: save them for salad dressings and marinades.

**Olives (azeitunas)** Spaniards are spoilt for choice when it comes to olives, and a bowl of olives is often served as the most simple tapas. Most other fruit contains large amounts of water; olives have oil. Over 50 varieties are grown, and over half those for eating, not pressing, come from Andalusia. Varieties include: *aragón*, small, smooth-skinned pale black with a hint of pink; *arbequiña*, tiny round pale green; *cacereña*, small, black, with firm flesh; *gordal*, very large, green, with a full flavor; and *manzanilla* (or Seville), small, green but fat, meaty and often stuffed with anchovies, pimentos, or tiny olives.

**Paprika (pimentón)** The orange-red color and sweet-to-hot earthy flavor of paprika finds its way into many Spanish dishes. Paprika is the finely ground powder of dried red sweet peppers; the degree of heat and intensity of color depends on the variety of sweet pepper. Hungarians are also major producers of paprika, but the Spanish variety is usually milder and slightly sweeter, although you will find some very hot Spanish paprika.

**Rice (arroz)** The short-grain rice grown in the coastal plains of the Levant is a staple ingredient found in most Spanish kitchens. It is the essential ingredient for Paella, as well as other rice preparations. Traditional Spanish rice cooking is unique in that the rice is neither covered nor stirred during cooking, resulting in dishes that are quite different from long-grain pilafs or creamy risottos, for example. All rice recipes, except Rice with Chorizo and Shrimp, have been tested with Calasparra rice, from Murcia, which is sold in Spanish food stores. You can substitute the short-grain rice sold in supermarkets as "Paella Rice;" risotto rice makes the result too mushy. Rice with Chorizo and Shrimp uses the new quick-cooking variety.

**Saffron (azafrán)** The golden hue and distinctive flavor of saffron is unmistakable in such classic Spanish dishes as Paella and Catalan Fish Stew. Saffron was introduced by the Moors when they conquered Spain in the early 8th century. It is made from the stigmas of the crocus and is the world's most expensive spice, because the labor-intensive process of removing the dusky red stigmas from the crocus plants (*Crocus sativus*) must be done by hand. It takes up to 75,000 stigmas to produce 1 lb/450 g saffron. Today sleepy villages in La Mancha produce an overwhelming amount of the world's supply. Harvesting the "red gold" takes place in October and the entire population of a village will become involved. Once the stigmas have been collected they are quickly toasted, after which, properly stored in an airtight container, the aroma will stay fresh for up to three years. Turmeric is often given as an acceptable, less expensive substitute for saffron, and although it gives a lovely golden color, its flavor and aroma are not at all similar.

**Turron (turrón)** This honey-flavored delicacy is similar to nougat. Its center of production since the times of the Moors has been Jijona, in the hills above Alicante. The two traditional versions, soft (*blando*) and hard (*duro*), have changed little over the centuries.

# TAPAS & APPETIZERS

One of the most pleasurable aspects of any visit to Spain is sampling the amazing array of tapas served in every village, town, or city. The preparation, eating, and enjoyment of tapas is a uniquely Spanish experience. Italians have *antipasti;* the French enjoy *hors d'oeuvres;* and a Greek *mezze* can consist of a dazzling display of appetizers, but no other culture has anything quite like tapas.

Tapas are an institution everywhere in Spain. These are tipbits of food for nibbling with drinks while chatting with friends, and range from a simple bowl of olives or almonds to more elaborate stuffed sweet peppers or golden tortilla.

Tapas can be made with seafood, meat, poultry, eggs, and vegetables, and served hot or chilled. As with most things Spanish, few conventions apply universally, but tapas bars usually open from lunchtime for several hours and then again in the evening when the work day finishes. For someone from Barcelona, for example, stopping off for tapas with colleagues will be a prelude to going home or on to a restaurant for the evening meal, whereas someone from Madrid might eat enough tapas to forgo another meal.

In most of the country the daily selection of tapas is displayed on a bar and a waiter puts your selection on a plate, for eating either standing up or seated at the bar or a table. In northern Spain, however, you help yourself and the bill is settled at the end, calculated on the number of small plates, toothpicks, or small wooden forks used to spear bite-size tidbits like broiled scallops or snails in oil. In Barcelona and other large cities long "fast-food" tapas bars thrive, with photographs of the range of tapas available on paper place mats—ideal for non-Spanish-speaking tourists, who can simply point and order!

The word "tapas" means a lid or cover, and it is thought tapas got their name from the days when a slice of bread covered with ham or cheese was placed on top of a wine or sherry glass to keep flies out while serving weary travelers on horseback. The price of simple tapas was once included in the cost of drinks, but that tradition, sadly, has all but died out.

The vast array of tapas fits within different categories. *Cosas de picar*, meaning little things to nibble, are finger food, such as Marinated Olives (see page 47), Paprika-Spiced Almonds (see page 50), Deep-Fried Green Chiles (see page 49), slices of Spanish Tortilla (see page 42), and Salads on Bread (see page 93). *Pinchos* are slightly more substantial and speared with toothpicks, such as Chorizo and Mushroom Kabobs (see page 74), Feisty Potatoes (see page 86), Chicken Livers with Sherry Glaze (see page 78), and Tiny Meatballs with Tomato Sauce (see page 77). *Cazuelas* are the small, brown

*It is thought tapas got their name from the days when a slice of bread covered with ham or cheese was placed on top of a wine or sherry glass to keep flies out*

earthenware dishes used by cooks all over Spain, so the tapas served in those dishes are likewise called *cazuelas*. These include Garlic Shrimp with Lemon and Parsley (see page 64) and Fava Beans with Ham (see page 81). *Raciones* are the more filling tapas, such as small kabobs, a selection of which will easily substitute for a meal.

Overleaf *Spain is so much more than sun and sandy beaches and exhibits an immense diversity of landscape*

# spanish tortilla
## *tortilla española*

*There is hardly a tapas bar in Spain that doesn't serve this simple, but delicious, set, thick omelet, and there can't be many Spanish cooks who don't make it look effortless as they turn out a golden tortilla. Generations ago it was said that country girls could improve their chance of marrying early by making an excellent tortilla.*

*This classic recipe, with only the simple ingredients of eggs, potatoes, and onion, is also known as* tortilla española. *Other tortilla names, however, give a clue to where they come from and what they include:* tortilla murciana *contains red bell peppers and tomatoes;* tortilla a la catalana *features the local* butifarra *sausage and beans;* tortilla de berenjenas *is an Andalusian eggplant version.*

**MAKES 8–10 SLICES**

$^1/_2$ **cup olive oil**

**1 lb 5 oz/600 g potatoes, peeled and sliced thinly**

**1 large onion, sliced thinly**

**6 large eggs**

**salt and pepper**

**flat-leaf parsley, to garnish**

1 Heat a 10-inch/25-cm skillet, preferably nonstick, over high heat. Add the oil and heat. Reduce the heat, then add the potatoes and onion and cook for 15–20 minutes until the potatoes are tender.

2 Beat the eggs in a large bowl and season generously with salt and pepper. Drain the potatoes and onion through a strainer over a heatproof bowl to reserve the oil. Very gently stir the vegetables into the eggs; set aside for 10 minutes.

3 Use a wooden spoon or spatula to remove any crusty bits stuck to the bottom of the skillet. Reheat the skillet over medium-high heat with 4 tablespoons of the reserved oil. Add the egg mixture and smooth the surface, pressing the potatoes and onions into an even layer.

4 Cook for about 5 minutes, shaking the skillet occasionally, until the base is set. Use a spatula to loosen the side of the tortilla. Place a large plate over the top and carefully invert the skillet and plate together* so the tortilla drops onto the plate.

5 Add 1 tablespoon of the remaining reserved oil to the skillet and swirl round. Carefully slide the tortilla back into the skillet, cooked side up. Run the spatula round the tortilla, to tuck in the edge.

6 Continue cooking for about 3 minutes until the eggs are set and the base is golden brown. Remove the skillet from the heat and slide the tortilla onto a plate. Let stand for at least 5 minutes before cutting. Serve warm or at room temperature.

*\*cook's tip*
If you are uncomfortable about inverting the tortilla, finish cooking it under a medium-high broiler, about 4 inches/10 cm from the heat source, until the runny egg mixture on top is set. The tortilla will not, however, have its characteristic "rounded" edge.

# oven-baked tortilla
## *tortilla al horno*

*In Madrid's tapas bars you could be served this
simply in 1-inch/2.5-cm squares with toothpicks for
picking up, while in other parts of Spain the squares
might be presented on bread slices.*

**MAKES 48 PIECES**

olive oil

1 large garlic clove, crushed

4 scallions, white and green parts chopped finely

1 green bell pepper, cored, seeded, and diced finely

1 red bell pepper, cored, seeded, and diced finely

6 oz/175 g potato, boiled, peeled, and diced

5 large eggs

generous ¹/₃ cup sour cream

1¹/₂ cups freshly grated Spanish Roncal cheese,
   or use Cheddar or Parmesan

3 tbsp chopped fresh chives

salt and pepper

1 Line a 7 x 10-inch/18 x 25-cm shallow ovenproof pan
with foil and brush with the oil; set aside.

2 Put a little oil, the garlic, scallions, and bell peppers
in a skillet and cook over medium heat, stirring, for
about 10 minutes until the onions are soft, but not
brown. Remove from the heat and let cool. Stir in
the potato.

3 Beat the eggs, sour cream, cheese, and chives
together in a large bowl. Stir the cooled vegetables
into the bowl and season with salt and pepper to taste.

4 Pour the mixture into the shallow pan and smooth
over the top. Bake in an oven preheated to
375°F/190°C for 30–40 minutes until golden brown,
puffed, and set in the center. Remove from the oven
and let cool and set. Run a spatula round the edge, then
invert onto a cutting board, browned side up; peel off
the foil. If the surface looks a little runny, put it under a
medium broiler to dry out.

5 Let cool completely. Trim the edges if necessary,
then cut into 48 squares. Serve on a platter with
wooden toothpicks, or secure each square to a slice
of bread.

# tomato bread
### *pa amb tomàquet*

*It is most unusual to have a meal in Barcelona that doesn't start with* Pa amb Tomàquet, *whether you are in a tapas bar, restaurant, or a private home. This is one of the classics of the region.*

**sliced bread or French loaf**
**tomatoes**
**garlic, optional**
**olive oil, optional**

1 At its simplest, slices of bread are simply rubbed with half a fresh juicy tomato. If the bread is soft, you can toast it first. Other options are to flavor it with garlic, or drizzle olive oil over the top.

*variation*
For a more substantial snack, serve tomato bread with a plate of thinly sliced serrano ham and Manchego cheese, and let guests assemble open sandwiches.

# marinated olives

## *azeitunas aliñadas*

*A Spanish cook is just as likely to buy marinated olives as to prepare his or her own, as the choice is so vast with endless flavor combinations. Markets and supermarkets always offer a huge selection of flavored olives, along with other vegetables, such as chiles and the long, sweet, Mediterranean-style sweet peppers. When you don't have so much choice, however, a jar of these is handy to have in the cupboard, to serve with drinks.*

**FILLS A 2-CUP PRESERVING JAR**

**1 cup green pimiento-stuffed Spanish olives in brine, rinsed**

**1 cup black Spanish olives in brine, rinsed**

**2 oz/55 g broiled and peeled sweet pepper (see page 74), sliced thinly**

**2 thin lemon slices**

**2 sprigs of fresh thyme**

**1 bay leaf**

**1 dried red chile**

**$\frac{1}{2}$ tsp fennel seeds**

**$\frac{1}{2}$ tsp coriander seeds, cracked lightly**

**extra virgin olive oil***

1 Place the olives, sweet pepper strips, lemon slices, thyme, bay leaf, chile, and fennel and coriander seeds in a 2-cup preserving jar, making sure the ingredients are well mixed. Pour over enough oil to cover. Seal the jar and set aside at room temperature for at least 2 weeks before using.

*\*cook's tips*
Do not add sliced garlic to an oil marinade such as this, because of the possibility of botulism infection. If you want a garlic flavor, use a commercially prepared garlic-flavored olive oil instead.

If you store the marinade in the fridge, the oil will become cloudy, but it clears again as it returns to room temperature.

# olives and anchovies
## *azeitunas y boquerones*

*You could be served this stylish tapas with drinks in a fashionable Barcelona restaurant. It is simplicity itself, and a chance to use your best extra virgin olive oil, the flavor of which is lost in cooking. In fact, this tapas is a wonderful example of Spanish fast food—all the ingredients will be in the kitchen cupboard. Another quick and easy example is to secure a marinated anchovy fillet round an olive. Precise quantities are not important.*

**seasoned anchovy fillets packaged in vegetable oil
(found in Spanish food stores)**
**Marinated Olives (see page 47)**
**small white pickled onions**
**extra virgin olive oil**

1 Separate the anchovies into individual fillets, then arrange on a plate with the olives and onions.

2 Drizzle with the best extra virgin olive oil and serve with plenty of toothpicks to spear the individual ingredients while you chat over drinks.

# deep-fried green chiles
## *pimientos fritos*

*Any sweet or hot chile peppers can be quickly deep-fried, and the stubby* pimientos de Padrón, *from the vegetable gardens south of Santiago de Compostela in Galicia, make an intriguing tapas to nibble with drinks when fried whole. You will find them in Spanish food stores and some supermarkets sold in 9-oz/250-g bags. They have a fresh chile taste, without much heat—except every bag seems to include one searingly hot chile, and you won't know which it is until you bite into it.*

**EACH BAG OF CHILES SERVES 4–6**
olive oil
sweet or hot green chiles
sea salt

1 Heat 3 inches/7.5 cm of oil in a heavy-bottom pan until it reaches 375°F/190°C, or until a day-old cube of bread turns brown in 30 seconds.

2 Rinse the chiles and pat them very dry with paper towels. Drop them in the hot oil for no longer than 20 seconds until they turn bright green and the skins blister.

3 Remove with a slotted spoon and drain well on crumpled paper towels. Sprinkle with sea salt and serve at once.

*variation*
For a more elaborate tapas, top a thin slice of bread with a fried egg, yolk side up. Secure the egg to the bread by skewering the set white to the bread with a toothpick with a fried *pimiento de Padrón* on it.

# paprika-spiced almonds
## *almendras al pimentón*

Almonds in a seemingly endless variety of
preparations are a popular Spanish snack with
drinks. They are often included in a selection of tapas
or served with sherry or wine in many wine or
cocktail bars. Sometimes the almonds will be simply
blanched without any extra flavorings, while other
times they will be pan-fried in olive oil and sprinkled
with coarse sea salt or coated with very finely
ground salt. This version adds the piquant flavor of
paprika. These almonds will keep for up to 3 days in
an airtight container.

**MAKES 1 LB 2 OZ/500 G; SERVES 4–6**

1 1/2 tbsp coarse sea salt

1/2 tsp smoked sweet Spanish paprika, or hot paprika,
 to taste

3 1/2 cups blanched almonds*

extra virgin olive oil

1 Put the sea salt and paprika in a mortar and grind
 with the pestle to a fine powder, or use a mini spice
blender (the amount is too small to process in a
full-size processor).

2 Place the almonds on a baking sheet and toast in
 a preheated oven, 400°F/200°C, for 8–10 minutes,
stirring occasionally, until golden brown and giving off
a toasted aroma: watch carefully after 7 minutes
because they burn quickly. Immediately pour into a
heatproof bowl.

3 Drizzle over about 1 tablespoon of oil and stir to
 ensure all the nuts are lightly and evenly coated;
add extra oil, if necessary. Sprinkle with the salt and
paprika mixture and stir again. Transfer to a small bowl
and serve at room temperature.

*cook's tip

It is best, and more economical, to buy unblanched
almonds and blanch them as and when required,
because they start to dry out as soon as the thin,
brown skin is removed. Put the unblanched almonds
in a heatproof bowl. Pour over boiling water and let
stand for 1 minute. Drain well, then pat dry and slip
off the skins.

# pickled mackerel 53
## *caballa en escabeche*

**SERVES 4–6**

8 fresh mackerel fillets

1¼ cups extra virgin olive oil

2 large red onions, sliced thinly

2 carrots, peeled and sliced

2 bay leaves

2 garlic cloves, sliced thinly

2 dried red chiles

1 fennel bulb, halved and sliced thinly

1¼ cups sherry vinegar

1½ tbsp coriander seeds

salt and pepper

toasted French bread slices, to serve

1 Place the mackerel fillets, skin-side up, on a broiler rack and brush lightly with a little of the oil. Broil under a medium-high broiler, 4 inches/10 cm from the heat source, for 4–6 minutes until the skins become brown and crispy and the flesh flakes easily; set aside.

2 Heat the remaining oil in a large skillet. Add the onions and cook for about 5 minutes until soft, but not brown. Add the remaining ingredients and let simmer for 10 minutes, or until the carrots are tender.

3 Flake the mackerel flesh into large pieces, removing the skin and tiny bones. Place the mackerel pieces in a preserving jar and pour over the onion, carrot, and fennel mixture. (The jar should accommodate everything packed in quite tightly with the minimum air gap at the top once the vegetable mixture has been poured in.) Let cool completely, then cover tightly and let chill for at least 24 hours and up to 5 days. Serve the pieces of mackerel on toasted slices of French bread with a little of the oil drizzled over.

Alternatively, serve the mackerel and its pickled vegetables as a first-course salad.

*variation*
This pickling brine is equally delicious with broiled cod or hake fillets, broiled and shelled mussels, or pan-fried tuna or swordfish steaks.

*Tapas bars and restaurants serving the real food of Spain are often tucked away from the obvious tourist haunts*

# pan-fried pickled angler fish

## *rape escabechado frito*

**SERVES 4–6**

1¼ lb/600 g angler fish

2½–3½ cups extra virgin olive oil

6 shallots, sliced thinly

2 carrots, peeled and sliced

1 fennel bulb, halved and sliced thinly

2 bay leaves

2 garlic cloves, sliced thinly

½ tsp dried red pepper flakes, or to taste

1¼ cups white wine vinegar

salt and pepper

1½ tbsp coriander seeds

lemon wedges, to serve

*for the batter*

scant 1 cup all-purpose flour, plus about 4 tablespoons
   extra for dusting

½ tsp salt

1 egg, separated

generous ¾ cup ale

1 tbsp olive oil

1 Remove the thin membrane covering the angler fish, then rinse the tail and pat it dry. Cut the tail lengthwise on either side of the central bone, then remove the bone and discard. Cut the angler fish flesh crosswise into ½-inch/1-cm slices.

2 Heat 4 tablespoons of the oil in a large skillet over medium heat. Add as many angler fish slices as will fit in a single layer and cook for 2 minutes. Turn over and continue for about 4 minutes, or until the slices are just cooked through and flake easily. Drain well on paper towels. Transfer to a nonmetallic bowl and set aside.

3 Heat scant 1¼ cups oil in the same skillet. Add the shallots and cook for 3 minutes until softened, but not browned. Stir in the carrots, fennel, bay leaves, garlic, red pepper flakes, vinegar, and salt and pepper.

Bring to a boil, then reduce the heat and let simmer for 8 minutes. Stir in the coriander seeds and continue simmering for 2 minutes, or until the carrots are tender.

4 Pour the hot mixture over the angler fish and set aside until completely cool. Cover and let chill for at least 24 hours and up to 5 days.

5 Make the batter 30 minutes before you plan to cook. Sift the flour and salt into a large bowl and make a well in the center. Add the egg yolk and generous ⅓ cup of the ale and gradually whisk the flour into the liquid to form a thick mixture. Stir in the oil and as much of the remaining ale to make a thick, smooth batter. Cover and let stand for 30 minutes.

6 Remove the angler fish pieces from the marinade and pat dry on paper towels; set aside. Heat enough oil for deep-frying in a large heavy-bottom pan until it sizzles—this takes about 40 seconds. Meanwhile, whisk the egg white until stiff peaks form. Stir the batter, then fold in the egg white.

7 Sift the remaining 4 tablespoons flour onto a plate and season to taste with salt and pepper. Roll the pieces of fish in it, shaking off the excess flour. Dip the angler fish pieces in the batter, then drop in the oil. Work in batches if necessary, to avoid overcrowding the pan. Cook for 3–4 minutes until golden. Remove and drain well on paper towels. Continue until all the fish is cooked, reheating the oil between batches.

8 Serve hot with lemon wedges for squeezing over the fish.

# salt cod fritters with spinach
## *buñelos de bacalao con espinacas*

*You need to allow 48 hours for soaking the dried salt cod for this dish. If you can't find dried salt cod in the supermarket, try Spanish or Caribbean food stores.*

**MAKES ABOUT 16**

**9 oz/250 g dried salt cod in 1 piece**

*for the batter*

**scant 1 cup all-purpose flour**

**1 tsp baking powder**

**¹/₄ tsp salt**

**1 large egg, beaten lightly**

**about ²/₃ cup milk**

**2 lemon slices**

**2 fresh parsley sprigs**

**1 bay leaf**

**¹/₂ tbsp garlic-flavored olive oil**

**scant 2 cups baby spinach, rinsed**

**¹/₄ tsp smoked sweet, mild, or hot Spanish paprika, to taste**

**olive oil**

**coarse sea salt, optional**

**1 quantity Garlic Mayonnaise (see page 232), to serve**

1 Place the dried salt cod in a large bowl, cover with cold water, and let soak for 48 hours, changing the water at least 3 times.

2 Meanwhile, make the batter. Sift the flour, baking powder, and salt into a large bowl and make a well. Mix the egg with generous ¹/₃ cup of the milk and pour into the well in the flour, stirring to make a smooth batter with a thick coating consistency. If it seems too thick, gradually stir in the remaining milk; set aside for at least 1 hour.

3 After the salt cod has soaked, transfer it to a large skillet. Add the lemon slices, parsley sprigs, bay leaf, and enough water to cover and bring to a boil. Reduce the heat and let simmer for 30–45 minutes until the fish is tender and flakes easily.

4 Meanwhile, prepare the spinach. Heat the oil in a small pan over medium heat. Add the spinach with just its rinsing water clinging to the leaves and cook for 3–4 minutes until wilted.

5 Drain the spinach in a strainer, using the back of a spoon to press out any excess. Finely chop the spinach, then stir it into the batter with the paprika.

6 Remove the fish from the water and flake the flesh into fine pieces, removing all the skin and tiny bones. Stir the flesh into the batter.

7 Heat 2 inches/5 cm of oil in a heavy-bottom skillet until it reaches 375°F/190°C or until a day-old cube of bread turns brown in 30 seconds. Use a greased tablespoon or measuring spoon to drop spoonfuls of the batter into the oil and cook for 8–10 minutes until golden brown. Work in batches to avoid crowding the skillet. Use a slotted spoon to transfer the fritters to paper towels to drain and sprinkle with sea salt, if using.

8 Serve hot or at room temperature with Garlic Mayonnaise for dipping.

# broiled sardines
## *sardinas asados*

*You will find this simple preparation is traditional all along Spain's Mediterranean coast, where the fish are prepared straight off the boats, often grilled over hot coals. Usually these sardines are served simply with lemon wedges for squeezing over the hot fish. Or, serve them with freshly prepared Garlic Mayonnaise (see page 232). An Orange and Fennel Salad (see page 109) complements the sardines for a summer lunch.*

*For a really robust flavor, insert an anchovy fillet in each fish cavity before broiling.*

**SERVES 4–6**

**2 tbsp garlic-flavored olive oil**

**12 fresh sardines, deheaded, cleaned, backbone removed\***

**coarse sea salt and pepper**

**lemon wedges, to serve**

1 Preheat the broiler to high and brush the broiler rack with a little of the garlic-flavored oil. Brush the sardines with the oil and arrange in a single layer on the broiler rack. Sprinkle with salt and pepper to taste.

2 Broil about 4 inches/10 cm from the heat for 3 minutes, or until the skin becomes crisp. Use kitchen tongs to turn the sardines over and brush with more oil and sprinkle with salt and pepper. Continue broiling for 2–3 minutes until the flesh flakes easily and the skin is crisp. Serve at once.

*\*cook's tips*

Look for firm fish with shiny skin and clear, bright eyes. Sardines are best cooked on the day of purchase, and should be refrigerated until they are broiled.

Fish merchants will prepare the sardines, but it is easy to do at home. Working with one sardine at a time, hold it firmly in one hand and snap off the head with your other hand, pulling downward. This should remove most of the guts with the head, but use a finger to remove any innards that remain. You can then use your thumb and index finger to grasp the top of the backbone and pull it toward you to remove. Rinse well and pat dry with paper towels.

# olives wrapped with anchovies
### *azeitunas envueltos de anchoas*

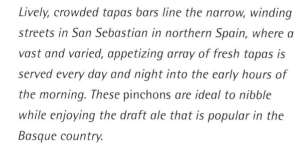

*Lively, crowded tapas bars line the narrow, winding streets in San Sebastian in northern Spain, where a vast and varied, appetizing array of fresh tapas is served every day and night into the early hours of the morning. These* pinchons *are ideal to nibble while enjoying the draft ale that is popular in the Basque country.*

**MAKES 12**
**12 anchovy fillets in oil, drained**
**24 pimiento-stuffed green olives in oil, drained**

1 Thinly slice each anchovy fillet lengthwise. Wrap a half fillet round the center of each olive, overlapping the ends, and secure with a wooden toothpick. Repeat with another olive and anchovy fillet half and slide onto the toothpick. Continue until all the ingredients are used, and you have 12 *pinchons* with 2 anchovy-wrapped olives on each toothpick.

*variation*
Instead of using pimiento-stuffed olives, stuff pitted green or black olives with a blanched anchovy sliver. Proceed with the recipe as above.

*Spain's Mediterranean and Atlantic waters offer up a plentiful supply of fish and seafood all year round*

# shrimp wrapped in ham 63
*gambas envueltos en jamón*

*Only make the dressing for this recipe when tomatoes are at their summer peak and bursting with flavor. Otherwise, serve the cooled shrimp with a bowl of Garlic Mayonnaise (see page 232), Romesco Sauce (see page 233), or Mojo Sauce (see page 84) for dipping.*

**MAKES 16**

*for the Tomato-Caper Dressing*

**2 tomatoes, peeled and seeded***

**1 small red onion, chopped very finely**

**4 tbsp very finely chopped fresh parsley**

**1 tbsp capers in brine, drained, rinsed, and chopped**

**finely grated rind of 1 large lemon**

**4 tbsp extra virgin olive oil**

**1 tbsp sherry vinegar**

**16 thin slices serrano ham or prosciutto**

**16 uncooked jumbo shrimp, shelled and deveined (see page 64), tails left on**

**extra virgin olive oil**

1 First, make the dressing. Finely chop the prepared tomato flesh and put it in a bowl. Add the onion, parsley, capers, and lemon rind, and gently toss together. Combine the oil and vinegar and add to the other ingredients; set aside until required.

2 Wrap a slice of ham round each shrimp and rub with a little of the oil. Place the shrimp in a heatproof dish large enough to hold them in a single layer. Bake in a preheated oven, 325°F/160°C, for 10 minutes.

3 Transfer the shrimp to a serving platter and spoon the tomato-caper dressing over. Serve at once, or let cool to room temperature.

*\*cook's tip*

To peel and seed tomatoes, remove the stems, and cut a small cross in the top of each one. Put the tomatoes into a heatproof bowl, pour over enough boiling water to cover, and let stand for 30 seconds. Use a slotted spoon to transfer to a bowl of iced water. Working with 1 tomato at a time, peel off the skin, then cut in half and use a teaspoon to scoop out the cores and seeds.

# garlic shrimp with lemon and parsley
## *gambas al ajillo con limón y perejil*

*Although the main ingredients in this simple dish are always the same—shrimp, garlic, and lemon—it is served in many guises: sometimes the shrimp will be unshelled; sometimes the heads and tails are left on; chiles and parsley are optional ingredients. This dish is best served hot, but the shrimp can also be taken out of the oil, left to cool, then served chilled.*

**SERVES 6**

**60 uncooked large shrimp, thawed if using**
   **frozen**

**²/₃ cup olive oil**

**6 garlic cloves, sliced thinly**

**3 dried hot red chiles, optional**

**6 tbsp freshly squeezed lemon juice**

**6 tbsp very finely chopped fresh parsley**

**French bread, to serve**

1 Shell and devein* the shrimp and remove the heads, leaving the tails on. Pat the shrimp dry.

2 Heat the oil in a large, deep sauté pan or skillet. Add the garlic and chiles, if using, and stir round until they start to sizzle. Add the shrimp and cook until they turn pink and curl.

3 Use a slotted spoon to transfer the shrimp to warm earthenware bowls. Sprinkle each bowl with lemon juice and parsley. Serve at once with plenty of bread to mop up the juices.

*\*cook's tip*
To devein shrimp, use a fine-bladed knife to slice along the back from the head end to the tail, then remove the thin, black intestine.

*Churches are a prominent feature of the Spanish landscape*

# sweet peppers stuffed with crab salad     67
## *pimientos del piquillo rellenos de ensalada de cangrejo*

*Most Spanish kitchens contain at least 1 jar or
can of sweet pimientos del piquillo, 3-inch/7.5-cm
long red sweet peppers that have been roasted,
peeled, and seeded. Sometimes they are also sold
sliced, so make sure you buy the whole ones,
preserved in oil or brine, for this recipe.*

**MAKES 16**

*for the Crab Salad*

**8¹/₂ oz/240 g crabmeat, drained and squeezed dry**

**1 red bell pepper, broiled, peeled (see page 74),
   and chopped**

**about 2 tbsp fresh lemon juice**

**salt and pepper**

**⁷/₈ cup cream cheese**

**16 pimientos del piquillo, drained, or freshly roasted
   sweet peppers\*, tops cut off**

**chopped fresh parsley, to garnish**

1 First make the crab salad. Pick over the crabmeat
and remove any bits of shell. Put half the crabmeat
in a food processor with the prepared red bell pepper,
1¹/₂ tablespoons of the lemon juice, and seasoning to
taste. Process until well blended, then transfer to a bowl.
Flake and stir in the cream cheese and remaining
crabmeat. Taste and add extra lemon juice, if required.

2 Pat dry the *pimientos del piquillo* and scoop out any
seeds that remain in the tips. Use a small spoon to
divide the crab salad equally between the sweet
peppers, stuffing them generously. Arrange on a large
serving dish or individual plates, cover and let chill until
required. Just before serving, sprinkle the stuffed
peppers with the chopped parsley.

*\*cook's tip*

If you can't find *pimientos del piquillo*, and have to
roast the peppers yourself, use 16 of the long, sweet
Mediterranean variety, not bell peppers. If, however, bell
peppers are the only ones you can find, cut 4–6 into
wedges and spread the crab salad along each wedge.

# flat bread with vegetables and clams
## *coca mallorquina*

**SERVES 4–6**

*for the dough*

2⅝ cups strong white flour, plus extra for kneading

1 package active dry yeast

1 tsp salt

½ tsp sugar

1 tbsp olive oil

1 tbsp dry white wine

1 cup warm water


2 tbsp extra virgin olive oil

4 large garlic cloves, crushed

2 large onions, sliced thinly

10 pimientos del piquillo (see page 67), drained, patted dry, and sliced thinly

9 oz/250 g shelled baby clams in brine (weight in jar), drained and rinsed

salt and pepper


1 To make the dough, stir the flour, yeast, salt, and sugar together in a bowl, making a well in the center. Add the oil and wine to the water, then pour ¾ cup of the liquid into the well. Gradually mix in the flour from the sides, adding the remaining liquid if necessary, until a soft dough forms.

2 Turn out the dough onto a lightly floured counter and knead until smooth. Shape the dough into a ball. Wash the bowl and rub the inside with oil. Return the dough to the bowl and roll it round so that it is lightly coated in oil. Cover the bowl tightly with plastic wrap and set aside in a warm place until the dough doubles in volume.

3 Heat the oil in a large, heavy-bottom skillet over medium-high heat. Reduce the heat and add the garlic and onions and cook slowly, stirring frequently, for 25 minutes, or until the onions are golden brown, but not burned.

4 Transfer the onions to a bowl and let cool. Add the pepper strips and clams to the bowl and stir together; set aside.

5 Knock back the dough and knead quickly on a lightly floured counter. Cover it with the upturned bowl and let stand for about 10 minutes, which will make it easier to roll out.

6 Heavily flour a 12¾ x 12¾-inch/32 x 32-cm shallow baking sheet. Roll out the dough to make a 13½-inch/34-cm square and transfer it to the baking sheet, rolling the edges to form a thin rim. Prick the base all over with a fork.

7 Spread the topping evenly over the dough and season with salt and pepper to taste. Bake in a preheated oven, 450°F/230°C, for 25 minutes, or until the rim is golden brown and the onions tips are slightly tinged. Transfer to a wire rack to cool completely. Cut into 12–16 slices.


Overleaf *Sausages and cured hams are among Spain's gastronomic delights*

# chickpeas and chorizo
## *garbanzos con chorizo*

1 Heat the oil in a large, heavy-bottom skillet over medium heat. Add the onion and garlic and cook, stirring occasionally, until the onion is softened, but not browned. Stir in the chorizo and continue cooking until it is heated through.

2 Tip the mixture into a bowl and stir in the chickpeas and peppers. Splash with sherry vinegar and season with salt and pepper to taste. Serve hot or at room temperature, generously sprinkled with parsley, with plenty of crusty bread.

**SERVES 4–6**

*For an authentic touch, present this simple tapas in individual earthenware casseroles called* cazuelas, *as it is served throughout Andalusia.*

4 tbsp olive oil

1 onion, chopped finely

1 large garlic clove, crushed

9 oz/250 g chorizo sausage in one piece, casing removed and cut into ¹/₂-inch/1-cm dice

14 oz/400 g canned chickpeas, drained and rinsed

6 pimientos del piquillo (see page 67), drained, patted dry, and sliced

1 tbsp sherry vinegar, or to taste

salt and pepper

finely chopped fresh parsley, to garnish

crusty bread slices, to serve

*Date palms are one reminder of Spain's Moorish past*

# chorizo & mushroom kabobs
## *pinchitos de chorizo y champiñones*

*These mini kabobs are an example of the type of tapas known as* pinchos, *or bite-size nibbles served on toothpicks.* Pinchos *aren't elaborate, but a step up from just putting out a bowl of almonds or olives to enjoy with drinks.*

**MAKES 25**

**2 tbsp olive oil**

**25 pieces of chorizo sausage, each about ¹/₂ inch/1 cm**
  **square (about 3¹/₂ oz/100 g)**

**25 white mushrooms, wiped and stalks removed**

**1 green bell pepper, broiled and peeled\*, and cut into**
  **25 squares**

1 Heat the oil in a skillet over medium-high heat. Add the chorizo and cook for 20 seconds, stirring. Add the mushrooms and continue cooking for an additional 1–2 minutes until the mushrooms start to brown and absorb the fat in the skillet.

2 Thread a green bell pepper square, a piece of chorizo, and a mushroom onto a wooden toothpick. Continue until all the ingredients are used. Serve hot or at room temperature.

*\*cook's tip*
To peel bell peppers, halve lengthwise, stem on, which makes removal of the core and seeds simpler. Broil, skin sides up, 2–3 inches/5–7.5 cm from the heat until charred all over. Remove from the heat and place in a plastic bag for 15 minutes, then rub or peel off the skins. Remove any cores and seeds. Alternatively, the peppers can be charred over a flame. Broiled and peeled, they can be kept for up to 5 days in the fridge, covered with olive oil.

*Stopping off for tapas is a daily feature of Spanish life, in the smartest cities or the humblest villages*

# tiny meatballs with tomato sauce
## *albondiguitas con salsa de tomates*

*Meatballs have been a regular feature of Spanish meals for hundreds of years, with the earliest recipes recorded in the thirteenth century.* Albondigas, *the Spanish word for meatball, comes from the Arabic* al-bunduq, *meaning hazelnut, presumably a reflection of the round shape. Meatballs are made in various sizes from beef, lamb, and pork, and sautéd or baked. Serve these individually with toothpicks for a light tapas\* with drinks, or thread 3 meatballs onto a toothpick for a more substantial snack, called a* racione.

*Mojo Sauce (see page 84) and Garlic Mayonnaise (see page 232) are also good with these.*

**MAKES ABOUT 60**

olive oil

1 red onion, chopped very finely

2¼ cups ground lamb

1 large egg, beaten

2 tsp freshly squeezed lemon juice

½ tsp ground cumin

pinch of cayenne pepper, to taste

2 tbsp very finely chopped fresh mint

salt and pepper

1¼ cups Tomato and Bell Pepper Sauce
  (see page 236), to serve

*\*cook's tip*

This is an ideal tapas to serve at a drinks party because the meatballs can be made ahead and both the sauce and meatballs can be served at room temperature. If you freeze the meatballs, allow 3 hours for them to thaw at room temperature.

1 Heat 1 tablespoon of oil in a skillet over medium heat. Add the onion and cook for about 5 minutes, stirring occasionally, until soft, but not brown.

2 Remove the skillet from the heat and let cool. Add the onion to the lamb with the egg, lemon juice, cumin, cayenne, mint, and salt and pepper to taste in a large bowl. Use your hands to squeeze all the ingredients together. Cook a small piece of the mixture and taste to see if the seasoning needs adjusting.

3 With wet hands, shape the mixture into about sixty ¾-inch/2-cm balls. Place on a baking sheet and let chill for at least 20 minutes.

4 When ready to cook, heat a small amount of oil in 1 or 2 large skillets (the exact amount of oil will depend on how much fat is in the lamb). Arrange the meatballs in a single layer, without overcrowding the skillet, and cook over medium-high heat for about 5 minutes until brown on the outside, but still pink inside. Work in batches if necessary, keeping the cooked meatballs warm while you cook the remainder.

5 Gently reheat the Tomato and Bell Pepper Sauce and serve with the meatballs for dipping. These are best served warm with reheated sauce, but they are also enjoyable at room temperature.

# chicken livers with sherry glaze
## *hígadillos al jerez*

**SERVES 4–6**

1 lb/450 g chicken livers, thawed if frozen

2 tbsp olive oil

2¹/₂ tbsp sherry vinegar

2 tbsp fino sherry

2 shallots, chopped finely

scant 1¹/₄ cups chicken stock

1 sprig of fresh thyme

2 tsp honey

pinch of cayenne pepper, to taste

salt and pepper

finely chopped fresh parsley, to garnish

*Anyone who visits only Spain's coastal resorts misses out on the huge diversity of the country, geographical and culinary*

1 Trim the chicken livers, removing any large veins or green spots; pat dry.

2 Heat the oil in a large skillet over medium-high heat. Add the chicken livers in a single layer and cook and stir for about 5 minutes until brown on the outside and just pink inside when you cut one open. Transfer the livers to a heatproof plate and keep warm in a low oven.

3 Add the vinegar, sherry, and shallots to the skillet and bring to a boil, scraping up any crispy bits from the bottom of the skillet. Add the chicken stock, thyme, honey, and cayenne, and let bubble until reduced to about 4 tablespoons.

4 Return the chicken livers to the skillet and heat through, stirring to coat with the glaze. Taste and adjust the seasoning and sprinkle with the parsley. Serve at once with wooden toothpicks.

# fava beans with ham
## *habas con jamón*

**SERVES 4–6**

³/₈ **cup fresh or frozen shelled fava beans**

**2 tbsp extra virgin olive oil**

**1 Spanish red onion, chopped very finely**

**1 slice medium-thick serrano ham or prosciutto, chopped**

**fresh parsley, chopped finely, to taste**

**salt and pepper**

**French bread, to serve**

1 Bring a large pan of salted water to a boil. Add the beans and continue to boil for 5–10 minutes until just tender. Drain and put in a bowl of cold water to stop further cooking. Unless the beans are young and tiny, peel off the outer skins.

2 Meanwhile, heat 1 tablespoon of the oil in a skillet over medium-high heat. Add the onion and cook for about 5 minutes until soft, but not brown. Add the beans.

3 Stir in the ham and parsley and check the seasoning; the meat is salty, so don't add salt until after tasting. Transfer to a serving bowl and drizzle with the remaining oil. Serve at room temperature with slices of French bread.

*The towns of the vast central plains of Spain blend seamlessly with the natural colors of the arid landscape*

# roasted asparagus with ham
*espárragos asados con jamón serrano*

*In late April, white and green asparagus appears on all menus, often as part of the menú del dia—the daily special—as Spaniards celebrate the harvest of one of their favorite vegetables. Asparagus is often steamed, but this technique prevents soggy spears, which can happen so quickly.*

*To serve as a tapas, arrange the asparagus spears on a platter round a small bowl of sauce so guests can casually dip the spears in the sauce. As a first course, arrange on individual plates with a little sauce spooned over.*

**SERVES 4–6**

**sea salt**

**24 spears fresh asparagus, woody ends snapped off**

**about 2 tbsp extra virgin olive oil**

**pepper**

**12 thin slices serrano ham or prosciutto, halved lengthwise**

**1 x quantity Romesco Sauce (see page 233) or**
**   Garlic Mayonnaise (see page 232), to serve**

1 Sprinkle a layer of sea salt over the bottom of a roasting pan that will hold the asparagus spears in a single layer. Brush the asparagus with the olive oil, then lay the spears in the roasting pan.

2 Roast in a preheated oven, 400°F/220°C, for 12–15 minutes until the asparagus is just tender when pierced with the tip of a knife. Remove from the oven and season to taste with freshly ground pepper.

3 As soon as you can hold the spears, wrap a piece of ham round each. Serve hot, warm, or at room temperature with a small bowl of Romesco Sauce or Garlic Mayonnaise for dipping.

# "wrinkled" potatoes with mojo sauce
## *papas arraguadas con mojo*

*Have plenty of chilled ales or water on hand when you serve this classic tapas from the Canary Islands. The potatoes are cooked in heavily salted water to resemble seawater, resulting in a thin film of salt on the skins. The salt and piquant sauce are very thirst-making. If you can't find new red-skinned potatoes, use new potatoes that hold their shape.*

**SERVES 4–6**

**generous ¹/₃ cup sea salt**

**24 small, new red-skinned potatoes, unpeeled and**
  **kept whole**

*for the Mojo Sauce*

**1¹/₂ oz/40 g day-old bread, crusts removed and torn**
  **into small pieces**

**2 large garlic cloves**

**¹/₂ tsp salt**

**1¹/₂ tbsp hot Spanish paprika**

**1 tbsp ground cumin**

**approx 2 tbsp red wine vinegar**

**approx 5 tbsp extra virgin olive oil**

**2 pimientos del piquillo (see page 67), preserved, drained**

1 Pour about 1 inch/2.5 cm water in a pan and stir in the sea salt. Add the potatoes and stir again: they do not have to be covered with water. Fold a clean dish towel to fit over the potatoes, then bring the water to a boil. Reduce the heat and let simmer for 20 minutes, or until the potatoes are tender, but still holding together.

2 Remove the dish towel and set aside. Drain the potatoes and return them to the empty pan. When the dish towel is cool enough to handle, wring the saltwater it contains into the pan. Put the pan over low heat and shake until the potatoes are dry and coated with a thin white film. Remove from the heat.

3 Meanwhile, make the Mojo Sauce. Put the bread in a bowl and add just enough water to cover; set aside for 5 minutes to soften. Use your hands to squeeze all the water from the bread. Use a mortar and pestle to mash the garlic and salt into a paste. Stir in the paprika and cumin. Transfer the mixture to a food processor. Add 2 tablespoons of vinegar and blend, then add the bread and 2 tablespoons of oil and blend again.

4 With the motor running, add the pepper pieces a few at a time until they are puréed and a sauce forms. Add more oil, if necessary, until the sauce is smooth and thick. Taste and adjust the seasoning, adding extra vinegar, if necessary.

5 To serve, cut the potatoes in half and spear with wooden toothpicks. Serve with a bowl of sauce on the side for dipping. The potatoes can be eaten hot or at room temperature.

# feisty potatoes
## *patatas bravas*

*This classic Catalan tapas is not called "feisty" for nothing—the sauce should be hot. You will find as many "authentic" recipes for this dish as there are cooks in Spain. Every cook has their own way: sometimes the potatoes are deep-fried, and often the garlic-flavored mayonnaise and chili oil are mixed together. This version is similar to the way they are served at Bar Tomás in the fashionable Barcelona neighborhood of Sarrià. The bar's* patatas bravas *have been voted among the city's best by* La Vanguardia *newspaper.*

**SERVES 6**

*for the Chili Oil*

²/₃ **cup olive oil**

**2 small, hot red chiles, slit**

**1 tsp hot Spanish paprika**

**1 x recipe Pan-Fried Potatoes (see page 247)**

**1 x recipe Garlic Mayonnaise (see page 232)**

1 To make the chili oil, heat the oil and chiles over high heat until the chiles start to sizzle. Remove from the heat and stir in the paprika. Set aside and let cool, then transfer to a pourer with a spout; do not strain.

2 Pan-fry the potatoes, and while they cook make the Garlic Mayonnaise.

3 To serve, divide the potatoes between 6 plates and add a spoonful of Garlic Mayonnaise to each. Drizzle with chili oil and serve warm or at room temperature. In Spain these are served with toothpicks.

# broiled eggplant dip
## *salsa de berenjenas*

**SERVES 6–8**

1 large eggplant, about 14 oz/400 g

olive oil

2 scallions, chopped finely

1 large garlic clove, crushed

2 tbsp finely chopped fresh parsley

salt and pepper

smoked sweet Spanish paprika, to garnish

French bread, to serve

1 Cut the eggplant into thick slices and sprinkle with salt to draw out any bitterness; set aside for 30 minutes, then rinse and pat dry.

2 Heat 4 tablespoons of the oil in a large skillet over medium-high heat. Add the eggplant slices and cook on both sides until soft and starting to brown. Remove from the skillet and set aside to cool. The slices will release the oil again as they cool.

3 Heat another tablespoon of oil in the skillet. Add the onions and garlic and cook for 3 minutes until the scallions become soft. Remove from the heat and set aside with the eggplant slices to cool.

4 Transfer all the ingredients to a food processor and process just until a coarse purée forms. Transfer to a serving bowl and stir in the parsley. Taste and adjust the seasoning, if necessary. Serve at once, or cover and let chill until 15 minutes before required. Sprinkle with paprika and serve with slices of French bread.

# traditional catalan salt cod salad
## *esqueixada*

*In fashionable Barcelona restaurants the salt cod in this classic salad is served in thin slices with finely diced tomato, sweet pepper, and olives sprinkled round the plate for the garnish\*. This more rustic version, however, is what you will find in country restaurants. Similar to ceviche, the fish in this recipe "cooks" in the acidity of the vinegar and lemon juice.*

**SERVES 4–6**

14 oz/400 g dried salt cod in one piece

6 scallions, sliced thinly on the diagonal

6 tbsp extra virgin olive oil

1 tbsp sherry vinegar

1 tbsp lemon juice

pepper

2 large red bell peppers, broiled, peeled (see page 74), seeded, and diced very finely

12 large black olives, pitted and sliced

2 large, juicy tomatoes, sliced thinly, to serve

2 tbsp very finely chopped fresh parsley, to garnish

1 Place the dried salt cod in a large bowl, cover with cold water, and let soak for at least 48 hours, changing the water occasionally.

2 Pat the salt cod very dry with paper towels and remove the skin and bones, then use your fingers to tear into fine shreds. Put in a large, nonmetallic bowl with the scallions, oil, vinegar, and lemon juice, and toss together. Season with freshly ground black pepper, cover, and put in the fridge to marinate for 3 hours.

3 Stir in the bell peppers and olives. Taste and adjust the seasoning, if necessary, remembering that the cod and olives might be salty. Arrange the tomato slices on a large platter or individual plates and spoon the salad on top. Sprinkle with parsley and serve.

*\*cook's tip*

To prepare the updated version of this salad, put the desalted salt cod in the freezer for about 30 minutes, then thinly slice. (If you try to slice the salt cod without freezing first, the slices will fall apart.)

*variations*

For a summer tapas, cut vine-ripened cherry tomatoes in half and use a teaspoon to scoop out the seeds. Sprinkle with sea salt and turn upside down on paper towels to drain for 30 minutes. Spoon the salad into the tomato halves and sprinkle with parsley.

The salt cod salad can also be used to stuff *pimientos del piquillo*, as in the recipe on page 67.

# pan-fried cheese
*queso frito*

*The tangy taste of this traditional Spanish sheep's cheese becomes more pronounced when the cheese is heated. These are best served as soon as they are cooked, but still enjoyable for up to 30 minutes, but any longer and the cheese becomes rubbery.*

**MAKES ABOUT 16**

7 oz/200 g Manchego cheese, in one piece

1 cup fresh fine white bread crumbs

1 tsp dried thyme

1 large egg

olive oil

1 x recipe Romesco Sauce (see page 233),
   to serve (optional)

1 Derind the cheese, then cut it into 16 wedge-shaped slices, each ¼–½ inch/0.5–1 cm thick; set aside. Mix the bread crumbs and thyme together on a plate and beat the egg in a soup plate.

2 Dip the cheese wedges, one by one, first in egg, then in bread crumbs, patting them on all over.

3 Heat ¼ inch/0.5 cm of oil in a heavy-bottom skillet over medium-high heat until a cube of day-old bread sizzles—this takes about 40 seconds. Add the cheese wedges and cook for about 30 seconds on each side until golden brown and crisp. Work in batches, if necessary, to avoid overcrowding the skillet.

4 As each wedge is cooked, remove it from the skillet, and drain on paper towels. Let cool slightly, then serve with a bowl of Romesco Sauce for dipping into, if liked.

*A monumental column makes an imposing silhouette against the sky at dusk*

# salads on bread

*montaditos*

Visit any tapas bar in northern Spain at lunchtime and you'll find plates of bread slices mounded with mayonnaise-based salads that look like two- or three-bite open sandwiches. Ensaladilla Rusa, *Russian Salad, diced potatoes, beans, carrots, and peas, is a popular, quickly assembled combination, as all Spanish supermarkets sell this prepared mix in jars.*

*Both of these salads also make a suitable stuffing for pimientos del piquillo (see page 67).*

**EACH SALAD QUANTITY MAKES 12–14 OPEN SANDWICHES**

*for the Potato Salad*

**7 oz/200 g new potatoes, scrubbed and boiled**

**¹/₂ tbsp white wine vinegar**

**salt and pepper**

**3–4 tbsp mayonnaise or Garlic Mayonnaise (see page 232)**

**2 hard-cooked eggs, shelled and chopped finely**

**2 scallions, white and green parts chopped finely**

**12–14 black olives, pitted and sliced, to garnish**

*for the Tuna Salad*

**7 oz/200 g canned tuna in olive oil, drained**

**4 tbsp mayonnaise or Garlic Mayonnaise (see page 232)**

**2 hard-cooked eggs, shelled and chopped finely**

**1 tomato, broiled and peeled, seeded (see page 63), and chopped very finely**

**2 tsp grated lemon rind, or to taste**

**cayenne pepper, to taste**

**salt and pepper**

**12–14 anchovy fillets in oil, drained, to garnish**

**24–28 slices from a long, thin loaf, say French bread, cut on a slight diagonal, about ¹/₄ inch/5 mm thick**

1 To make the potato salad, peel the potatoes as soon as they are cool enough to handle, then cut them into ¹/₄-inch/5-mm dice. Toss with the vinegar and season with salt and pepper to taste; set aside to cool completely. Stir in the mayonnaise, then fold in the chopped eggs and scallions. Taste and adjust the seasoning. Mound generously on the bread slices, then top each with olive slices.

2 To make the tuna salad, flake the drained tuna into a bowl. Stir in the mayonnaise, then fold in the hard-cooked eggs, tomato, lemon rind, and cayenne. Taste and adjust the seasoning if necessary. Mound generously on the bread slices, then top each with anchovy fillets.

# moorish zucchini salad

*ensalada de calabacines a la morisco*

*The combination of toasted pine nuts and plump raisins has featured in Spanish recipes since the Moors ruled the Iberian Peninsula from AD 711 to 1492.*

*This versatile chilled salad can be spooned onto bread slices as tapas, served as a first course on a bed of salad greens, or as an accompaniment for roast chicken as part of a summer buffet. Make this at least 4 hours in advance, so the flavors blend.*

**SERVES 4–6**

about 4 tbsp olive oil

1 large garlic clove, halved

18 oz/500 g small zucchinis, sliced thinly*

1/2 cup pine nuts

1/3 cup raisins

3 tbsp finely chopped mint leaves (not spearmint or peppermint)

about 2 tbsp lemon juice, or to taste

salt and pepper

1 Heat the oil in a large skillet over medium heat. Add the garlic and let it cook until golden to flavor the oil, then remove and discard. Add the zucchinis and cook, stirring until just tender. Immediately remove from the skillet and transfer to a large serving bowl.

2 Add the pine nuts, raisins, mint, lemon juice, and salt and pepper to taste and stir together. Taste, and add more oil, lemon juice and seasoning, if necessary.

3 Set aside and let cool completely. Cover and let chill for at least 3 1/2 hours. Remove from the fridge 10 minutes before serving.

*\*cook's tip*

This salad is best made with young, tender zucchinis no more than 1 inch/2.5 cm thick. If using older, larger zucchinis, cut them in half or quarters lengthwise first, then slice thinly.

*variation*

For a more robust flavor, chop 4 drained anchovy fillets in oil and add in step 2.

# figs with blue cheese
## *higos con queso picós*

*A delicious combination of sweet–savory flavors, and a stylish first course for a dinner party. Cabrales, matured in limestone caves, is Spain's best-known blue cheese, but Picós is a milder version that works well in this recipe. Usually made from sheep's milk, it can, however, contain three types of milk and is traditionally wrapped in grape leaves.*

**SERVES 6**
*for the caramelized almonds*
**¹/₂ cup superfine sugar**
**generous ³/₄ cup whole almonds, blanched or unblanched**

**12 ripe figs**
**12 oz/350 g Spanish blue cheese, such as Picós, crumbled**
**extra virgin olive oil**

1 First make the caramelized almonds. Put the sugar in a pan over medium-high heat and stir until the sugar melts and turns golden brown and bubbles: do not stir once the mixture starts to bubble. Remove from the heat and add the almonds one at a time and quickly turn with a fork until coated; if the caramel hardens, return the pan to the heat. Transfer each almond to a lightly buttered baking sheet once it is coated. Let stand until cool and firm*.

2 To serve, slice the figs in half and arrange 4 halves on each plate. Coarsely chop the almonds by hand. Place a mound of blue cheese on each plate and sprinkle with chopped almonds. Drizzle the figs very lightly with the oil.

*variation*
Walnut halves can also be caramelized and used in this recipe.

*\*cook's tip*
Store the nuts in an airtight jar for up to 3 days until required; any longer and they become soft.

*Pavement tables for leisurely lunches are an eye-catching feature of any Spanish city*

# gazpacho

*gazpacho*

1 Put the tomatoes, red bell peppers, 2 tablespoons of sherry vinegar, the oil, and sugar in a food processor and process until blended and as smooth or chunky as you like. Cover and let chill for at least 4 hours before serving. Taste and adjust the seasoning, adding extra vinegar if necessary*.

2 To serve, ladle the soup into bowls and add 1 or 2 ice cubes to each. Put a selection of garnishes in bowls and let everyone add their own.

*cook's tip*
Cold dulls flavors, so more seasoning will be needed than for a soup served warm. For this reason, taste and adjust the seasoning after chilling the soup.

*This is one of the classic chilled soups that is as refreshing as fruit juice on a hot summer's day.*

**SERVES 4–6**
1 lb 2 oz/500 g large, juicy tomatoes, peeled, seeded (see page 63), and chopped
3 large, ripe red bell peppers, cored, seeded, and chopped
about 2 tbsp sherry vinegar
4 tbsp olive oil
pinch of sugar
salt and pepper

*to serve*
ice cubes
finely diced red bell pepper
finely diced green bell pepper
finely diced yellow bell pepper
finely diced seeded cucumber
finely chopped hard-cooked eggs
croutons fried in garlic-flavored olive oil

*The heat of the midday sun in much of Spain slows the pace of life, and necessitates refreshing food and drink*

# roasted tomato soup
## *sopa de tomates asados*

*Andalusian and Canary Island farmers grow many of the tomatoes Europeans eat throughout the year. Even in those sunny climates, however, the seemingly never-ending polytunnels can produce pale and insipid specimens that benefit from the flavor boost provided by the tomato paste and sherry in this recipe. This richly flavored soup is best served hot, but it can also be served well chilled. (It is, however, completely different from the uncooked and refreshing Gazpacho on page 99 in both its texture and flavor.)*

**SERVES 4–6**

**2 lb/900 g large, juicy tomatoes, halved**

**2 tbsp butter**

**1 tbsp olive oil**

**1 large onion, sliced**

**2–3 tbsp tomato paste, depending on the flavor of the tomatoes**

**3¹/₂ cups vegetable stock**

**2 tbsp amontillado sherry**

**¹/₂ tsp sugar**

**salt and pepper**

**crusty bread, to serve**

1 Preheat the broiler to high. Place the tomatoes, cut sides up, on a baking sheet and broil about 4 inches/10 cm from the heat for 5 minutes, or until just starting to char on the edges.

2 Meanwhile, melt the butter with the oil in a large pan or flameproof casserole over medium heat. Add the onion and cook for 5 minutes, stirring occasionally. Stir in the tomato paste and continue cooking about 2 minutes.

3 Add the tomatoes, stock, sherry, sugar, and salt and pepper to taste to the pan and stir. Bring to a boil, then reduce the heat to low and let simmer, covered, for about 20 minutes until the tomatoes are reduced to a pulp.

4 Process the soup through a mouli* into a large bowl. Return to the rinsed pan and reheat, uncovered, simmering 10 minutes, or until the desired consistency is achieved. Ladle into individual bowls and serve with plenty of bread*.

*cook's tips*

If you don't possess a mouli, purée the soup in a food processor or blender then work through a fine strainer to achieve the smooth texture.

When serving chilled, swirl 1 tablespoon of sour cream in each bowl and sprinkle with parsley.

# chilled garlic soup
*ajo blanco*

**SERVES 4–6**

1 lb 2 oz/500 g day-old country-style white bread,
   crusts removed and torn
5 large garlic cloves, halved
$^1/_2$ cup extra virgin olive oil, plus a little extra
   to garnish
4–5 tbsp sherry vinegar, to taste
3 cups ground almonds
5 cups water, chilled
salt and white pepper
seedless white grapes, to garnish

1 Put the bread in a bowl with just enough cold water
to cover and let soak for 15 minutes. Squeeze the
bread dry and transfer it to a food processor.

2 Add the garlic, oil, 4 tablespoons of sherry vinegar,
and the ground almonds to the food processor with
scant 1$^1/_4$ cups of the water and process until blended.

3 With the motor running, slowly pour in the
remaining water until a smooth soup forms. Taste
and add extra sherry vinegar if necessary. Cover and let
chill for at least 4 hours.

4 To serve, stir well and adjust the seasoning if
necessary. Ladle into bowls and float grapes on top
with a drizzle of olive oil.

*The architecture of old Spain proudly bears the hallmarks
of its Moorish past*

# stuffed bell peppers
## *pimientos rellenos*

*This is an all-purpose vegetable dish—as well as being served as a tapas, a first course, or a light lunch dish with a sliced tomato salad, these bell peppers also make a good accompaniment to roast poultry and meat.*

**MAKES 6**

**6 tbsp olive oil, plus a little extra for rubbing on peppers**

**2 onions, chopped finely**

**2 garlic cloves, crushed**

**²/₃ cup Spanish short-grain rice**

**¹/₃ cup raisins**

**¹/₂ cup pine nuts**

**3 tbsp fresh parsley, chopped finely**

**salt and pepper**

**1 tbsp tomato paste dissolved in 3 cups hot water**

**4–6 red, green, or yellow bell peppers (or a mix of colors), or 6 of the long, Mediterranean variety**

1 Heat the oil in a shallow, heavy-bottom flameproof casserole. Add the onions and cook for about 3 minutes. Add the garlic and cook for an additional 2 minutes, or until the onion is soft but not brown.

2 Stir in the rice, raisins, and pine nuts until all are coated in the oil, then add half the parsley and salt and pepper to taste. Stir in the dissolved tomato paste and bring to a boil. Reduce the heat and let simmer, uncovered, for 20 minutes, shaking the casserole frequently, or until the rice is tender, the liquid is absorbed and small holes appear on the surface: watch carefully because the raisins can catch and burn easily. Stir in the remaining parsley, then set aside and let cool slightly.

3 While the rice is simmering, cut the top off each bell pepper and set aside. Remove the core and seeds from each pepper*.

4 Divide the stuffing equally between the bell peppers. Use wooden toothpicks to secure the tops back in place. Lightly rub each bell pepper with oil and arrange in a single layer in a baking dish. Bake in a preheated oven, 400°F/200°C, for 30 minutes, or until the bell peppers are tender. Serve hot or let cool to room temperature.

*\*cook's tip*
If you are using the pointed, Mediterranean variety of sweet pepper, a melon baller, teaspoon or small paring knife makes it easier to remove all the seeds.

# basque scrambled eggs
*piperrada*

SERVES 4–6

olive oil

1 large onion, chopped finely

1 large red bell pepper, cored, seeded, and chopped

1 large green bell pepper, cored, seeded, and chopped

2 large tomatoes, peeled, seeded (see page 63),
and chopped

2 oz/55 g chorizo sausage, sliced thinly, casings
removed, if preferred

3 tbsp butter

10 large eggs, beaten lightly

salt and pepper

4–6 thick slices country-style bread, toasted, to serve

1 Heat 2 tablespoons of oil in a large, heavy-bottom skillet over medium-high heat. Add the onion and bell peppers and cook for about 5 minutes, or until the vegetables are soft, but not brown. Add the tomatoes and heat through. Transfer to a plate and keep warm in a preheated low oven.

2 Add another tablespoon of oil to the skillet. Add the chorizo and cook for 30 seconds, just to warm through and flavor the oil. Add the sausage to the reserved vegetables.

3 There should be about 2 tablespoons of oil in the skillet, so add a little extra, if necessary, to make up the amount. Add the butter and let melt. Season the eggs with salt and pepper, then add them to the skillet. Scramble the eggs until they are cooked to the desired degree of firmness. Add extra seasoning to taste. Return the vegetables to the skillet and stir through. Serve at once with hot toast.

*Few urban dwellings in Spain have gardens, but a balcony is perfect for enjoying the evening atmosphere*

# orange and fennel salad
## *ensalada de naranjas y hinojo*

**SERVES 4**

4 large, juicy oranges

1 large fennel bulb, sliced very thinly

1 mild white onion, sliced finely

2 tbsp extra virgin olive oil

12 plump black olives, pitted and sliced thinly

1 fresh red chile, seeded and sliced very thinly (optional)

finely chopped fresh parsley

French bread, to serve

1 Finely grate the rind from the oranges into a bowl; set aside. Using a small serrated knife, remove all the white pith from the oranges, working over a bowl to catch the juices. Cut the oranges horizontally into thin slices.

2 Toss the orange slices with the fennel and onion slices. Whisk the oil into the reserved orange juice, then spoon over the oranges. Sprinkle the olive slices over the top, add the chile, if using, then sprinkle with the orange rind and parsley. Serve with slices of French bread.

*variations*

• For a more substantial meal, add soaked and cooked salt cod (see page 56).

• Garnet-red blood oranges look stunning.

• Juicy dark grapes make an interesting alternative to the olives.

*The Plaza de Catalunya in Barcelona is a quieter part of this thronging city*

# chorizo and quail's eggs
## *chorizo y huevos de codorniz*

1 Preheat the broiler to high. Arrange the slices of bread on a baking sheet and broil until golden brown on both sides.

2 Cut or fold the chorizo slices to fit on the toasts; set aside.

3 Heat a thin layer of oil in a large skillet over medium heat until a cube of day-old bread sizzles—this takes about 40 seconds. Break the eggs into the skillet* and cook, spooning the fat over the yolks, until the whites are set and the yolks are cooked to your liking.

4 Remove the cooked eggs from the skillet and drain on paper towels. Immediately transfer to the chorizo-topped toasts and dust with paprika. Sprinkle with salt and pepper to taste, and serve at once.

*cook's tip
Despite their delicate appearance, quail's eggs can be difficult to crack because of a relatively thick membrane under the shell. It is useful to have a pair of scissors handy to cut through the membrane as you break the eggs into the skillet.

*There isn't anything traditional about this recipe. This is an example of the new style of tapas served in Euro-chic hotel cocktail lounges in Barcelona and Madrid—ideal for enjoying with a chilled flûte of cava.*

**MAKES 12**

**12 slices French bread, sliced on the diagonal, about ¹/₄ inch/5 mm thick**

**about 1¹/₂ oz/40 g cured, ready-to-eat chorizo, cut into 12 thin slices**

**olive oil**

**12 quail's eggs**

**mild paprika**

**salt and pepper**

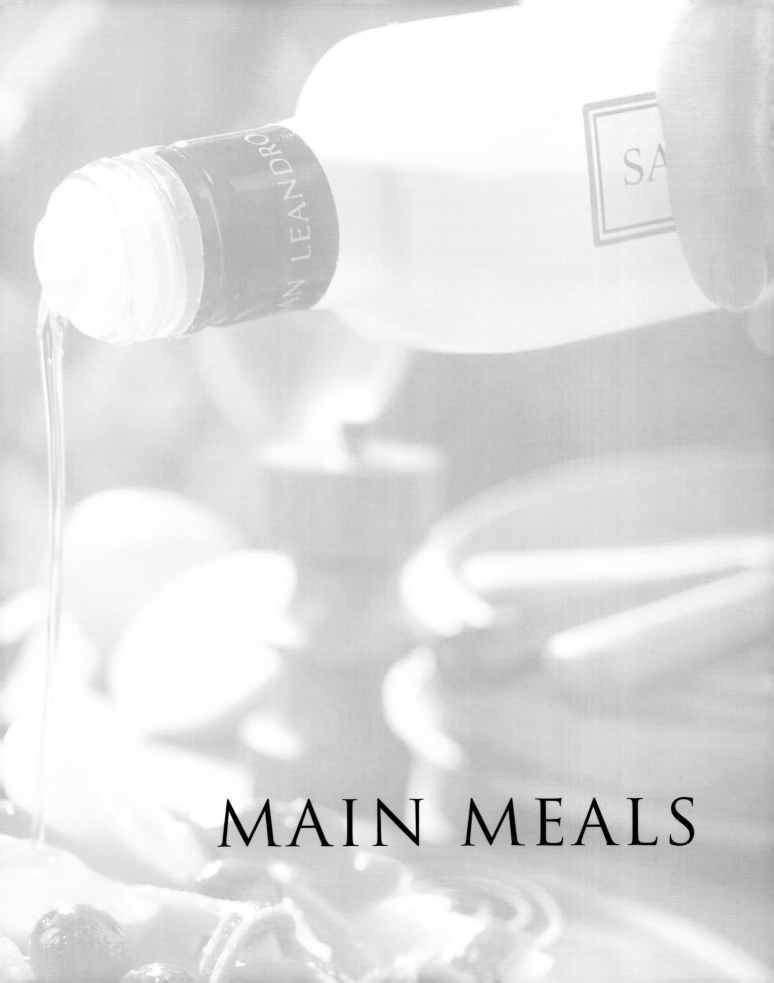

# MAIN MEALS

Who can think of Spain without conjuring up images of the magnificent seafood dishes offered up by the Mediterranean and the country's other coastal waters? Yet, the Spaniards are great meat-eaters as well, so the choice of main meals is varied. Spanish main courses are served simply and not heavily sauced as they tend to be in neighboring France.

Spanish cooks usually serve vegetables as an integral part of the main course or as a separate course, rather than on the side, a presentation reflected in dishes such as Chicken Thighs with Fava Beans and Mushrooms (see page 126), Veal with Pickled Vegetables (see page 139), Roasted Garlic-and-Rosemary Lamb with Potatoes (see page 143), and Cod with Spinach (see page 169).

Paella (see page 121), the saffron-flavored rice dish from Valencia, is always popular with Spaniards and tourists alike. The recipe in this chapter includes chicken portions and seafood, but the ingredients can be varied to accommodate whatever you have to hand. Rice and seafood have an affinity, and Black Rice (see page 122), colored and flavored by black squid ink, is another Mediterranean favorite.

Restaurants along the Mediterranean specialize in deep-frying almost anything that was swimming the day before, and you can re-create holiday meals at home with Deep-Fried Seafood (see page 159).

Yet not all of Spain is hot and sunny all the time, and Pork with Bell Peppers (see page 140) and Lamb Stew with Chickpeas (see page 144) are examples of hearty, richly flavored Spanish stews that provide warmth during cold winters.

Quails with Grapes (see page 135) is a dish inspired by the Spanish passion for game shooting. It is rich and sweet, and makes an impressive main course for a dinner party.

For quick and easy midweek family meals, try Meatballs with Peas (see page 136), Rice with Chorizo and Shrimp (see page 125), and Sausages with Lentils (see page 147).

Spanish cuisine scarcely accommodates vegetarians who do not include fish or seafood in their diets. Fortunately, however, egg dishes are always on the menu, and Basque Scrambled Eggs (see page 106) and Eggs on Vegetables (see page 177), minus the chorizo, are both suitable and delicious. Tortilla (see page 42) is another traditional dish that is always available. Fresh salads are of course an option for vegetarians, and the Broiled Bell Pepper Salad (see page 178) from Murcia makes a filling main course served with country-style crusty bread. Although Spanish gardens supply out-of-season vegetables to the rest of Europe, seasonal produce is greatly valued in Spain, so salads are a magnificent feast of vibrant colors and full flavors. During the summer months,

*Seasonal produce is valued in Spain so salads are a magnificent feast of vibrant colors and full flavors*

as temperatures rise, salads and barbecues become the favored meals for relaxed eating.

Most main courses will be accompanied by a bottle of wine, although Spaniards are less obsessed with "rules" such as only white wine with seafood and red wine with meat than, say, the French. More likely, the wine will be whatever is produced locally and it will have a natural affinity with local dishes. However, in the Basque Country and other regions along the Bay of Biscay, a glass of the locally produced cider will be the drink of choice.

Overleaf *The Royal Palace, in Madrid, is spectacular against the skyline*

Unlike risotto, the rice for a good paella is not sticky with sauce, yet each grain should be moist with oil. Stirring disrupts the way the rice cooks. Gradually lowering the heat as the liquid reduces, and giving the paella pan a shake, will help to prevent the rice sticking.

# paella
## paella

SERVES 6–8

2 pinches of saffron threads

1$^7/_8$ cup Spanish short-grain rice

16 live mussels

about 6 tbsp olive oil

6–8 unboned chicken thighs, excess fat removed, skin on

5 oz/140 g chorizo sausage, cut into $^1/_4$-inch/5-mm slices, casings removed

2 large onions, chopped

4 large garlic cloves, crushed

1 tsp mild or hot Spanish paprika, to taste

3$^1/_2$ oz/100 g green beans, chopped

$^7/_8$ cup frozen peas

5 cups fish, chicken, or vegetable stock

salt and pepper

16 uncooked shrimp, shelled and deveined (see page 64)

2 sweet red peppers, broiled, peeled (see page 74), and sliced

3 tbsp fresh parsley, chopped finely

1 Put the saffron threads in a small bowl and pour in 4 tablespoons of hot water; set aside. Put the rice in a strainer and rinse until the water runs clear; set aside. Scrub the mussels, removing any beards, and discard any with cracked shells or open ones that do not close when tapped; set aside.

2 Heat 3 tablespoons of oil in a 12-inch/30-cm paella pan or flameproof casserole over medium-high heat. Add the chicken thighs, skin sides down, and cook for 5 minutes, or until golden and crispy. Transfer to a bowl.

3 Add the chorizo to the paella pan and cook for 1 minute until it starts to crisp. Add to the chicken.

4 Heat another 3 tablespoons of oil in the paella pan. Add the onions and cook for 2 minutes, then add the garlic and paprika and cook for an additional 3 minutes until the onions are soft, but not brown.

5 Add the drained rice, beans, and peas to the paella pan and stir until coated in oil. Return the chicken thighs and chorizo and any accumulated juices to the casserole. Stir in the stock, saffron liquid, and salt and pepper and bring to a boil, stirring.

6 Reduce the heat to low and let simmer, without stirring, for 15 minutes* or until the rice is almost tender and most of the liquid is absorbed.

7 Arrange the mussels, shrimp, and sweet pepper strips on top, cover the casserole, and continue simmering, without stirring, for about 5 minutes until the shrimp become pink and the mussels open.

8 Discard any mussels that are not open. Taste and adjust the seasoning. Sprinkle with the parsley and serve at once.

*cook's tip

The first time you make this, preheat the oven to 375°F/190°C while the paella simmers. Heat sources are not consistent on stoves, so it is hard to say how long it takes for the liquid to be absorbed. If there is too much liquid on the surface, put the dish in the oven, cover, and bake for 10 minutes, or until very little liquid remains.

# black rice
## *arroz negro*

*The easiest way to approach this popular Mediterranean recipe is to buy cleaned squid bodies prepared by a fish merchant. Sachets of squid ink can be bought separately. If, however, you do buy a whole squid, the pearly blue-gray sac containing the ink, which gives the dish its characteristic gray-black color, is located under the tentacles, and it must be handled gently so it doesn't break.\* Use good-quality fish stock, rather than a cube.*

### SERVES 4–6

1⁷/₈ cup Spanish short-grain rice

6 tbsp olive oil

1 large onion, sliced finely

2 large garlic cloves, crushed

2 tomatoes, broiled, peeled, seeded (see page 63), and chopped finely

1 prepared squid body,\* cut into ¹/₄-inch/5-mm rings (tentacles set aside, if available)

4 cups fish stock

ink sac from squid, or a sachet of squid ink

salt and pepper

12 large uncooked shrimp, shelled and deveined (see page 64)

squid tentacles, if available

2 red bell peppers, broiled, peeled (see page 74), seeded and sliced

1 x recipe Garlic Mayonnaise (see page 232), to serve

1 Put the rice in a strainer and rinse until the water runs clear; set aside.

2 Heat the oil in a large, shallow casserole or skillet over medium-high heat. Add the onion and cook for 3 minutes, then add the garlic cloves and cook for an additional 2 minutes until the onion is soft, but not brown.

3 Add the tomatoes and let simmer until they are very soft. Add the squid rings and cook quickly until they turn opaque.

4 Add the rice and stir until it is coated in oil. Pour in the stock, squid ink, and salt and pepper to taste and bring to a boil. Reduce the heat and let simmer for 15 minutes, uncovered and without stirring, but shaking the skillet frequently, until most of the stock is absorbed and small holes appear on the surface.

5 Lightly stir in the shrimp, squid tentacles, if using, and bell peppers. Cover the skillet and continue simmering for about 5 minutes until the shrimp turn pink and the tentacles turn opaque and curl.

6 Taste and adjust the seasoning. Serve with Garlic Mayonnaise on the side of each plate.

*\*cook's tip*

To prepare squid, cut off the tentacles just in front of the eyes; discard the hard beak, but set aside the tentacles if they are to be used. Hold the body in one hand and use your other hand to pull out the head, which will bring the innards along as well. Remove and set aside the ink sac, but discard the rest of the innards. Use your fingers to pull out the transparent, quill-like bone in the cavity. Rub off the outer membrane, and cut off and discard the fins. Rinse the squid body and pat dry. You can use the body cavity whole for stuffing, or slice, as for the recipe here.

# rice with chorizo and shrimp
## *arroz con chorizo y gambas*

The 21st century is well established in Spanish supermarkets, with a seemingly endless array of preserved and prepared ingredients that help make home cooking quick and easy. One example of changing cooking habits is the use of long-grain, quick-cooking rice. If you can't find the Spanish variety, use any quick-cooking rice for this simple midweek supper dish.

**SERVES 4**

**2 tbsp olive oil**

**1 large onion, chopped**

**1 red bell pepper, cored, seeded, and chopped**

**1 green bell pepper, cored, seeded, and chopped**

**2 large garlic cloves, crushed**

**1 large tomato, chopped**

**scant 1 cup easy-cook Spanish rice**

**salt and pepper**

**7 oz/200 g chorizo sausage, cut into $^1/_4$–inch/5-mm**
**slices, casings removed**

**2 cups vegetable, fish, or chicken stock**

**1 lb/450 g large uncooked shrimp, shelled and deveined**
**(see page 64)**

**2 tbsp finely chopped fresh parsley, to garnish**

1 Heat the oil in a large, lidded skillet over medium-high heat. Add the onion and bell peppers and cook for 2 minutes. Add the garlic and continue cooking, stirring occasionally, for 3 minutes, or until the onion and bell peppers are soft, but not brown.

2 Add the tomato, rice, and salt and pepper to taste and continue cooking for 2 minutes.

3 Stir in the chorizo, then the stock and bring to a boil. Reduce the heat to low, cover, and let simmer for 15 minutes until the rice is tender, but still moist.

4 Stir in the shrimp, cover, and cook for about 5 minutes until they turn pink and the liquid has been absorbed: if the rice remains too moist, let simmer for an additional 2 minutes, uncovered. Taste and adjust the seasoning if necessary. Sprinkle with parsley and serve.

# chicken thighs with fava beans and mushrooms
*muslos de pollo con habas y champiñones*

*Many people have been put off fava beans by the thought of their unappetizing and tough gray skins. Unless the beans are young and tiny, it is best to blanch them before cooking.*

**SERVES 4**

3¹⁄₂ cups fresh or frozen shelled fava beans

olive oil

8 unboned chicken thighs, excess fat removed, skin on

1 large onion, sliced finely

1 large garlic clove, crushed

1 lb 2 oz/500 g cremini mushrooms, wiped and
   sliced thickly

salt and pepper

scant 2¹⁄₂ cups chicken stock

finely chopped fresh parsley, to garnish

Pan-Fried Potatoes (see page 247), to serve

1 To blanch the beans, bring a large pan of salted water to a boil, add the beans, and continue boiling for 5–10 minutes until just tender. Drain and put in a bowl of cold water to stop further cooking. Peel off the outer skins; set aside.

2 Heat 2 tablespoons of the oil in a large, lidded skillet or flameproof casserole over medium-high heat. Add 4 chicken thighs, skin sides down, and cook for 5 minutes, or until the skins are crisp and golden. Remove from the skillet and keep warm and cook the remaining thighs, adding a little extra oil if necessary.

3 Drain off all but 2 tablespoons of the fat in the skillet. Add the onion and cook for 3 minutes, then add the garlic and continue cooking for 5 minutes until the onion is golden. Stir in the mushrooms and salt and pepper to taste and continue cooking for 2 minutes, or until the mushrooms absorb all the fat and start to give off their juices.

4 Return the chicken thighs to the skillet, skin sides up. Pour in the chicken stock and bring to a boil. Reduce the heat to low, cover tightly, and let simmer for 15 minutes.

5 Add the beans and continue simmering for 5 minutes until the beans are tender* and the chicken juices run clear when a thigh is pierced. Taste and adjust the seasoning. Sprinkle with parsley and serve with Pan-Fried Potatoes.

*\*cook's tip*
Unblanched fava beans can take up to 20 minutes to cook, depending on their age. Frozen beans can be added straight from the freezer in Step 5 and simmered for 5 minutes until tender.

# chicken with garlic 129
## *pollo ajo*

*You'll find versions of this simple dish at country restaurants all over Spain. The slow, gentle cooking of the garlic removes the pungency and makes it meltingly tender—mash it on the side of your plate to spread on the chicken pieces. Serve this with Pan-Fried Potatoes (see page 247).*

**SERVES 4–6**

**4 tbsp all-purpose flour**

**Spanish paprika, either hot or smoked sweet, to taste**

**salt and pepper**

**1 large chicken, about 3³/₄ lb/1.75 kg, cut into 8 pieces, rinsed, and patted dry**

**4–6 tbsp olive oil**

**24 large garlic cloves, peeled and halved**

**scant 2 cups chicken stock, preferably homemade**

**4 tbsp dry white wine, such as white Rioja**

**2 sprigs fresh parsley, 1 bay leaf, and 1 sprig fresh thyme, tied together**

**fresh parsley and thyme leaves, to garnish**

1 Sift the flour onto a large plate and season with paprika and salt and pepper to taste. Dredge the chicken pieces with the flour on both sides, shaking off the excess.

2 Heat 4 tablespoons of the oil in a large, deep skillet or flameproof casserole over medium heat. Add the garlic pieces and cook, stirring frequently, for about 2 minutes to flavor the oil. Remove with a slotted spoon and set aside to drain on paper towels.

3 Add as many chicken pieces, skin-side down, as will fit in a single layer. (Work in batches if necessary, to avoid overcrowding the skillet, adding a little extra oil if necessary.) Cook for 5 minutes until the skin is golden brown. Turn over and cook for 5 minutes longer.

4 Pour off any excess oil. Return the garlic and chicken pieces to the skillet and add the chicken stock, wine, and herbs. Bring to a boil, then reduce the heat, cover, and let simmer for 20–25 minutes until the chicken is cooked through and tender and the garlic very soft.

5 Transfer the chicken pieces to a serving platter and keep warm. Bring the cooking liquid to a boil, with the garlic and herbs, and boil until reduced to about 1¹/₂ cups. Remove and discard the herbs. Taste and adjust the seasoning, if necessary.

6 Spoon the sauce and the garlic cloves over the chicken pieces. Garnish with the parsley and thyme, and serve.

# paprika chicken on a bed of onions and ham
## *pollo al pimentón sobre cebollas y jamón*

*Marinating chicken breasts in lemon juice is an old trick for tenderizing the flesh. For best results, leave the chicken in the marinade overnight.*

**SERVES 4**

**4 chicken breast fillets, skin on**

**²/₃ cup freshly squeezed lemon juice**

**1–1¹/₂ tsp mild or hot Spanish paprika, to taste**

**salt and pepper**

**about 2 tbsp olive oil**

**2¹/₂ oz/70 g serrano ham or prosciutto, diced**

**4 large onions, sliced thinly**

**¹/₂ cup dry white wine**

**¹/₂ cup chicken stock**

**fresh thyme or chopped fresh parsley, to garnish**

*The normally busy streets of Spanish towns may seem abandoned during the siesta*

1 To marinate the chicken, put the breasts in a nonmetallic bowl. Pour over the lemon juice and let marinate in the fridge overnight.

2 When you are ready to cook, remove the chicken breasts from the marinade and pat dry. Rub the skins with the paprika and salt and pepper to taste.

3 Heat 2 tablespoons of the oil in a large, lidded heavy-bottom skillet or flameproof casserole over medium-high heat. Add the chicken breasts, skin-sides down, and cook for 5 minutes, or until the skins are crisp and golden; remove from the skillet.

4 Stir the ham into the fat remaining in the skillet, cover, and cook for about 2 minutes until it renders any fat. Add the onions and continue cooking, stirring occasionally and adding a little extra oil if necessary. Cook for about 5 minutes until the onions are soft, but not brown.

5 Add the wine and stock and bring to a boil, stirring. Return the chicken breasts to the skillet and season with salt and pepper to taste. Reduce the heat, cover, and let simmer for 20 minutes, or until the chicken is cooked through and the juices run clear.

6 Transfer the chicken to a plate and keep warm in a preheated oven. Bring the sauce to a boil and let bubble until the juices reduce. Taste and adjust the seasoning. Divide the onion mixture between 4 warmed plates and arrange a chicken breast on top of each. Garnish with the herbs and serve at once.

# duck legs with olives
*muslos de pato con azeitunas*

*Duck features in recipes from Navarre, Catalonia, and Andalusia. This one is very simple to prepare.*

**SERVES 4**

4 duck legs, all visible fat trimmed off

1 lb 12 oz/800 g canned tomatoes, chopped

8 garlic cloves, peeled, but left whole

1 large onion, chopped

1 carrot, peeled and chopped finely

1 celery stalk, peeled and chopped finely

3 sprigs fresh thyme

generous ½ cup Spanish green olives stuffed with
    pimientos in brine, rinsed

salt and pepper

1 tsp finely grated orange rind

1 Put the duck legs in the bottom of a flameproof casserole or a large, heavy-bottom skillet with a tight-fitting lid. Add the tomatoes, garlic, onion, carrot, celery, thyme, and olives, and stir together. Season with salt and pepper to taste.

2 Turn the heat to high and cook, uncovered, until the ingredients start to bubble. Reduce the heat to low, cover tightly, and let simmer for 1¼–1½ hours until the duck is very tender. Check occasionally and add a little water if the mixture appears to be drying out.

3 When the duck is tender, transfer it to a serving platter, cover, and keep hot in a preheated warm oven. Leave the casserole uncovered, increase the heat to medium, and cook, stirring, for about 10 minutes until the mixture forms a sauce. Stir in the orange rind, then taste and adjust the seasoning if necessary.

4 Mash the tender garlic cloves with a fork and spread over the duck legs. Spoon the sauce over the top. Serve at once.

*Colorful architectural features are set off beautifully by an equally vivid sky*

*Shooting is a popular pastime in Spain, and an assortment of game dishes appear on many restaurant menus.*

**SERVES 4**

*for the Potato Pancake*

**1 lb 5 oz/600 g unpeeled potatoes**

**2¹/₂ tbsp unsalted butter or pork fat**

**1¹/₂ tbsp olive oil**

**4 tbsp olive oil**

**8 quails, cleaned**

**generous 1¹/₂ cups green seedless grapes**

**1 cup grape juice**

**2 cloves**

**about ²/₃ cup water**

**salt and pepper**

**2 tbsp Spanish brandy**

# quails with grapes
## *codornices con uvas*

135

1 First, parboil the potatoes for the pancake for 10 minutes. Drain and let cool completely, then peel, coarsely grate, and season with salt and pepper to taste; set aside.

2 Heat the oil in a heavy-bottom skillet or flameproof casserole large enough to hold the quail in a single layer over medium heat. Add the quail and cook on all sides until they are golden brown.

3 Add the grapes, grape juice, cloves, enough water to come halfway up the side of the quails, and salt and pepper to taste. Cover and let simmer for 20 minutes. Transfer the quails and all the juices to a roasting pan, unless cooking in a casserole, and sprinkle with brandy. Place in a preheated oven, 450°F/230°C, and roast, uncovered, for 10 minutes.

4 Meanwhile, to make the potato pancake, melt the butter or fat with the oil in a 12-inch/30-cm nonstick skillet over high heat. When the fat is hot, add the potato and spread into an even layer. Reduce the heat and let simmer for 10 minutes. Place a plate over the skillet and, wearing oven mitts, invert them so the potato pancake drops onto the plate. Slide the potato back into the skillet and continue cooking for 10 minutes, or until cooked through and crisp. Slide out of the skillet and cut into 4 wedges, and keep warm until the quail is ready.

5 Place a potato pancake wedge and 2 quails on each plate. Taste the grape sauce and adjust the seasoning if necessary. Spoon over the quails and serve.

# meatballs with peas
## *albondigas con guisantes*

**SERVES 4–6**

2¹/₄ cups lean ground beef

1 onion, grated

1 cup fresh white bread crumbs

1 egg, beaten lightly

2 tbsp fresh parsley, chopped finely

salt and pepper

olive oil

2 large onions, sliced thinly

1 x recipe Tomato and Bell Pepper Sauce (see page 236)

1¹/₂ cups frozen peas

1 Put the meat in a bowl with the grated onion, bread crumbs, egg, parsley, and salt and pepper to taste. Use your hands to squeeze all the ingredients together. Cook a small piece of the mixture and taste to see if the seasoning needs adjusting.

2 With wet hands, shape the mixture into 12 balls. Put on a plate and let chill for at least 20 minutes.

3 When ready to cook, heat a small amount of the oil in 1 or 2 large skillets: the exact amount needed will depend on how much fat there is in the beef. Arrange the meatballs in a single layer, without overcrowding, and cook, stirring, for about 5 minutes until brown on the outside; work in batches if necessary.

4 Set the meatballs aside and remove all but 2 tablespoons of oil from the skillet. Add the sliced onions and cook for about 5 minutes until soft, but not brown. Return the meatballs to the skillet.

5 Stir the Tomato and Bell Pepper Sauce into the skillet and bring to a boil, gently spooning the sauce and onions over the meatballs. Reduce the heat, cover, and let simmer for 20 minutes. Add the peas and continue simmering for 7–10 minutes until the peas are tender and the meatballs cooked through. Serve at once.

# veal with pickled vegetables

## *ternera con verduras en escabeche*

1 To make the vegetable *escabeche*, heat the oil in a skillet over medium heat. Add the shallots and saffron and cook for 5–7 minutes until the shallots start to caramelize. Add the carrots, beans, and cauliflower. Reduce the heat to very low, cover, and cook for 5–8 minutes until the vegetables are tender-crisp. Stir in the vinegar, coriander seeds, peppercorns, and bay leaf. Remove from the heat and let cool, unless you are serving the dish immediately.

*The* escabeche *mixture can be made up to two days in advance and stored in olive oil in a covered container in a fridge, and then reheated as the veal chops broil. It also goes well with broiled steaks, or pork chops, or roasted poultry.*

2 When ready to cook, lightly drizzle the chops with more oil and season with salt and pepper to taste. Place under a preheated hot broiler, about 4 inches/ 10 cm from the source of the heat, and broil for 3 minutes. Turn the chops over and broil for an additional 2 minutes if you like them cooked medium.

3 Transfer the chops to individual plates and spoon a little of the *escabeche* on the side of each. Sprinkle the vegetables with the chives, and drizzle with a little of the flavored oil. Serve at once.

**SERVES 4**

*for the vegetable* escabeche

²/₃ **cup olive oil**

**4 shallots, sliced**

**2 pinches of saffron threads**

**1 lb/450 g young carrots, peeled and sliced thinly**

**8 oz/225 g green beans, chopped small**

**8 oz/225 g tiny cauliflower florets**

**3 tbsp white wine vinegar**

**1 tsp coriander seeds, crushed**

**¹/₂ tsp black peppercorns, crushed**

**1 bay leaf, torn in half**

**4 veal loin chops, about 8 oz/225 g each and**
   **³/₄ inch/2 cm thick**

**salt and pepper**

**2 tbsp finely chopped fresh chives, to garnish**

**garlic–flavored olive oil, for drizzling**

*Spanish cities are richly endowed with palaces and monuments of civic pride*

# pork with bell peppers
## *espalda de cerdo al chilindrón*

*Cooking* al chilindrón *is popular throughout Spain, but it was originally from the northern regions of Navarre and Aragón, where the rugged conditions demanded hearty, full-flavored dishes. The dried chiles in this recipe provide a close-to-authentic fiery flavor, so for a milder dish, use dried* ñora *chiles. You need to marinate the pork for at least 8 hours, preferably overnight.*

### SERVES 4–6

2 lb/900 g pork shoulder, boned and trimmed, but left in
   1 piece

1 cup dry white wine

6 garlic cloves, crushed

2 dried ancho or pasila chiles

about 4 tbsp olive oil

2 large onions, chopped

4 red or green bell peppers, or a mixture, broiled, peeled
   (see page 74), seeded, and sliced

1/2 tsp hot paprika

1 lb 12 oz/800 g canned chopped tomatoes

2 sprigs fresh thyme

2 sprigs fresh parsley

salt and pepper

1 Place the pork in a nonmetallic bowl. Pour over the wine and add 4 of the garlic cloves. Cover with plastic wrap and let marinate in the fridge for at least 8 hours.

2 Put the chiles in a heatproof bowl and pour over enough boiling water to cover. Let stand for 20 minutes to soften, then seed and chop; set aside.

3 Heat 4 tablespoons of oil in a large, heavy-bottom flameproof casserole over medium-high heat. Add the onions and cook for 3 minutes, then add the remaining garlic cloves, chopped chile, bell pepper slices, and paprika, and cook for an additional 2 minutes until the onions are soft, but not brown. Use a slotted spoon to transfer the mixture to a plate, leaving as much oil as possible in the casserole.

4 Drain the pork, reserving the marinade, and pat dry. Add the pork to the casserole, and cook until brown on both sides.

5 Return the onion mixture to the casserole with the pork and stir in the reserved marinade, tomatoes with their juices, the herbs, and salt and pepper to taste. Bring to a boil, scraping any glazed bits from the bottom of the pan. Transfer the casserole to a preheated oven, 325°F/160°C, and cook for 1 hour, or until the pork is tender.

6 If the juices are too thin, remove the pork from the casserole and keep warm. Put the casserole over high heat and let the juices bubble until reduced to the desired consistency.

7 Taste and adjust the seasoning. Cut the pork into serving pieces and serve with the peppers and sauce from the casserole.

# roasted garlic-and-rosemary lamb with potatoes 143
## *cordero asado con ajo y romero*

*Wonderful aromas will fill the kitchen while this simple recipe from Aragon roasts. The northern region is known for its suckling lamb, with the tender flesh flavored by the animal grazing on wild herbs. For the full garlic flavor, the lamb needs to marinate for at least 2 hours.*

**SERVES 6–8**

**15 garlic cloves, unpeeled, but separated into cloves**

**olive oil**

**1 leg of lamb, about 3 lb/1.3 kg**

**handful of fresh, tender rosemary sprigs**

**salt and pepper**

**24 new potatoes, scrubbed, but left whole**

**scant 1¼ cups full-bodied red wine, say one from Rioja or Navarre**

1 Rub the garlic cloves with a little oil in your hands so they are coated. Place them in a small roasting pan and roast in a preheated oven, 400°F/200°C, for 20 minutes, or until very soft; cover the garlic with foil, shiny side in, if the cloves start to brown too much.

2 As soon as the garlic is cool enough to handle, peel the cloves. Use the back of a fork, or a mortar and pestle, to pound the garlic into a coarse paste with ½ teaspoon of oil. Make small incisions all over the lamb, then rub in the garlic paste. Let marinate for at least 2 hours in a cool place.

3 When you are ready to cook, place the lamb in a roasting pan on a bed of rosemary sprigs, and season with salt and pepper. Rub the potatoes with oil and place round the lamb. Sprinkle with more rosemary and season with salt and pepper to taste. Roast in a preheated oven, 450°F/230°C, for 10 minutes, then reduce the heat to 350°F/180°C for 15 minutes per 1 lb 2 oz/500 g plus an extra 15 minutes for medium, or until the temperature reaches 160°F/70°C on an internal meat thermometer.

4 Transfer the lamb to a carving plate and let stand for 10 minutes before carving. The potatoes should be tender at this point, but if not, return them to the oven in a separate dish while you deglaze the pan.

5 Set aside the rosemary sprigs and skim off any fat in the pan. Pour the wine into the pan and bring to a boil, scraping up any glazed bits from the bottom. Continue boiling until reduced to half. Taste and adjust the seasoning.

6 Slice the lamb and serve with the potatoes and juices spooned round.

# lamb stew with chickpeas
## *caldereta de cordero con garbanzos*

**SERVES 4–6**

olive oil

8 oz/225 g chorizo sausage, cut into ¹/₄-inch/5-mm
thick slices, casings removed

2 large onions, chopped

6 large garlic cloves, crushed

2 lb/900 g boned leg of lamb, cut into 2-inch/5-cm
chunks

scant 1¹/₄ cups lamb stock or water

¹/₂ cup red wine, such as Rioja or Tempranillo

2 tbsp sherry vinegar

1 lb 12 oz/800 g canned chopped tomatoes

salt and pepper

4 sprigs fresh thyme

2 bay leaves

¹/₂ tsp sweet Spanish paprika

1 lb 12 oz/800 g canned chickpeas, rinsed and drained

sprigs fresh thyme, to garnish

1 Heat 4 tablespoons of oil in a large, heavy-bottom flameproof casserole over medium-high heat. Reduce the heat, add the chorizo, and cook for 1 minute; set aside. Add the onions to the casserole and cook for 2 minutes, then add the garlic and continue cooking for 3 minutes, or until the onions are soft, but not brown. Remove from the casserole and set aside.

2 Heat an additional 2 tablespoons of oil in the casserole. Add the lamb cubes in a single layer without overcrowding the casserole, and cook until browned on each side; work in batches, if necessary.

3 Return the onion mixture to the casserole with all the lamb. Stir in the stock, wine, vinegar, tomatoes with their juices, and salt and pepper to taste. Bring to a boil, scraping any glazed bits from the bottom of the casserole. Reduce the heat and stir in the thyme, bay leaves, and paprika.

4 Transfer to a preheated oven, 325°F/160°C, and cook, covered, for 40–45 minutes until the lamb is tender. Stir in the chickpeas and return to the oven, uncovered, for 10 minutes*, or until they are heated through and the juices are reduced.

5 Taste and adjust the seasoning. Garnish with thyme and serve.

*cook's tip*
If the juices seem too thin, put the casserole on the stove and use a slotted spoon to remove the meat and chickpeas; keep warm. Bring the juices to a boil and boil until reduced; then return the other ingredients.

# sausages with lentils
## *salchichas merguez con lentejas*

*Although Algerian in origin, spicy merguez sausages have made their way into Spanish markets, and are ideal in this hearty pepper and lentil dish. Chorizo, cut into 1¹/₂-inch/4-cm cubes, is also suitable, as are other fresh pork, wild boar, or beef sausages.*

**SERVES 4–6**

2 tbsp olive oil

12 merguez sausages

2 onions, chopped finely

2 red bell peppers, cored, seeded, and chopped

1 orange or yellow bell pepper, cored, seeded. and chopped

scant 1¹/₂ cups small green lentils, rinsed

1 tsp dried thyme or marjoram

2 cups vegetable stock

salt and pepper

4 tbsp chopped fresh parsley

red wine vinegar, to serve

1 Heat the oil in a large, preferably nonstick, lidded skillet over medium-high heat. Add the sausages and cook, stirring frequently, for about 10 minutes until they are brown all over and cooked through; remove from the skillet and set aside.

2 Pour off all but 2 tablespoons of oil from the skillet. Add the onions and bell peppers and cook for about 5 minutes until soft, but not brown. Add the lentils and thyme or marjoram and stir until coated with oil.

3 Stir in the stock and bring to a boil. Reduce the heat, cover, and let simmer for about 30 minutes until the lentils are tender and the liquid is absorbed; if the lentils are tender, but too much liquid remains, uncover the skillet and let simmer until it evaporates. Season to taste with salt and pepper.

4 Return the sausages to the skillet and reheat. Stir in the parsley. Serve the sausages with lentils on the side, then splash a little red wine vinegar over each portion.

Left *The dry and dusty landscape of La Mancha provides excellent growing conditions for saffron, olives, and grapes*

Overleaf *The cook in Spain has a splendid choice of freshly landed fish and seafood*

# roast angler fish with romesco sauce
*rape asado con romesco*

*Serve this with Saffron Rice with Green Vegetables (see page 244) or Pan-Fried Potatoes (see page 247).*

**SERVES 4–6**

2 lb/900 g angler fish in 1 piece

2–3 slices serrano ham or prosciutto

olive oil

salt and pepper

1 x recipe Romesco Sauce (see page 233), to serve

1 Remove the thin membrane covering the angler fish, then rinse the tail and pat it dry. Wrap the ham round the angler fish and rub lightly with oil. Season with salt and pepper. Put on a baking sheet.

2 Roast the angler fish in a preheated oven, 400°F/200°C, for 20 minutes until the flesh is opaque and flakes easily: test by lifting off the ham along the central bone and cut a small amount of the flesh away from the bone to see if it flakes.

3 Cut through the ham to remove the central bone and produce 2 thick fillets. Cut each fillet into 2 or 3 pieces and arrange on a plate with a spoonful of Romesco Sauce. Serve at once.

*Spain has rich fishing grounds off both its Atlantic and Mediterranean coasts*

# spaghetti with shrimp
## *espaguetis con gambas*

*If only Italy comes to mind when you think of seafood pasta dishes, think again. Pasta and pizzas are popular in small, inexpensive restaurants throughout Spain, too. At the beach resort of La Manga, south of Alicante, dishes such as this one feature on many menus.*

**SERVES 4**

1 lb/450 g dried spaghetti

¹/₂ cup olive oil

6 garlic cloves, sliced thinly

1 lb/450 g medium uncooked shrimp, shelled
   and deveined (see page 64)

2 tbsp flat-leaf parsley, chopped finely,
   plus 2 tbsp extra for garnishing

¹/₂ cup dry white wine

4 tbsp freshly squeezed lemon juice

salt and pepper

1 Bring a large pan of salted water to a boil over high heat. Add the spaghetti, return the water to a boil, and continue boiling for 10 minutes (check the package instructions), or until tender.

2 Meanwhile, heat the oil in another large pan over medium heat. Add the garlic and cook until just golden brown. Add the shrimp and 2 tablespoons chopped parsley and stir. Add the wine and let simmer for 2 minutes. Stir in the lemon juice and continue simmering until the shrimp turn pink and curl.

3 Drain the spaghetti. Tip into the pan with the shrimp and toss. Add salt and pepper to taste.

4 Transfer to a large serving platter and sprinkle with the extra parsley. Serve at once.

*Gaudi's cathedral, Sagrada
Familia, in Barcelona*

# mussels with fennel

*mejillónes con hinojo*

**SERVES 4–6**

4 tbsp olive oil

2 large onions, sliced thinly

1 fennel bulb, trimmed and sliced thinly

2 large garlic cloves, chopped finely

1¹/₂ cups dry white wine, say a
    white Rioja

generous ¹/₃ cup fino sherry

14 oz/400 g canned tomatoes

pinch of sugar

salt and pepper

4 lb 8 oz/2 kg live mussels

handful finely chopped fresh parsley

1 Heat the oil in a large, heavy-bottom pan or stockpot over medium-high heat. Add the onions and fennel and cook for 3 minutes, stirring. Add the garlic and cook for an additional 2 minutes, or until the onions and fennel are soft, but not brown.

2 Add the wine and sherry and let them bubble until reduced by half. Add the tomatoes with their juices and bring to a boil, stirring. Add the sugar and salt and pepper to taste, reduce the heat, and let simmer for 5 minutes, uncovered.

3 Meanwhile, prepare the mussels. Cut off and discard any beards, then scrub any dirty shells. Discard any mussels with broken shells or open ones that do not close when tapped.

4 Reduce the heat under the pan to very low. Add the mussels, cover, and let simmer, shaking the pan frequently, for 4 minutes. Discard any mussels that have not opened; remove the remainder and divide them between 4 serving bowls. Re-cover the pan and continue simmering for an additional minute.

5 Stir the parsley into the juices in the pan. Taste and adjust the seasoning. Pour the juices over the bowls of mussels, and serve at once with plenty of bread for mopping up the juices.

# catalan fish stew
## *zarzuela*

1 Put the saffron threads in a heatproof bowl, add 4 tablespoons of boiling water; set aside to infuse.

2 Heat the oil in a large, heavy-bottom flameproof casserole over medium-high heat. Reduce the heat to low, add the onion, and cook for 10 minutes, or until golden, but not brown. Stir in the garlic, thyme, bay leaves, and red bell peppers and continue cooking for an additional 5 minutes, or until the bell peppers are soft and the onions have softened further.

3 Add the tomatoes and paprika and continue to simmer for 5 minutes, stirring frequently.

4 Stir in the fish stock, reserved saffron water, and ground almonds, and bring to a boil, stirring frequently. Reduce the heat and let simmer for 5–10 minutes until the sauce reduces and thickens. Add salt and pepper to taste.

5 Meanwhile, prepare the mussels and clams. Cut off and discard any beards from the mussels, then scrub any dirty shells.

6 Gently stir in the hake so it doesn't break up and add the shrimp, mussels, and clams. Reduce the heat to very low, cover the casserole, and let simmer for about 5 minutes until the hake is cooked through, the shrimp turn pink and the mussels and clams open; discard any mussels or clams that remain closed. Serve at once with plenty of thick, crusty bread for soaking up the juices.

*This traditional recipe takes its name from the Spanish word meaning "variety show," which reflects the variety of seafood you will find in the stew. Although the fish and shellfish will vary with the day's catch, saffron, almonds, garlic, and tomatoes typically feature.*

**SERVES 4–6**

**large pinch of saffron threads**

**6 tbsp olive oil**

**1 large onion, chopped**

**2 garlic cloves, chopped finely**

**1 1/2 tbsp chopped fresh thyme leaves**

**2 bay leaves**

**2 red bell peppers, cored, seeded, and chopped coarsely**

**1 lb 12 oz/800 g canned chopped tomatoes**

**1 tsp sweet smoked paprika**

**scant 1 1/4 cups fish stock**

**1 cup blanched almonds, toasted (see page 50) and ground finely**

**salt and pepper**

**12–16 live mussels with uncracked, tightly closed shells (discard any open ones that do not close when tapped)**

**12–16 live clams with uncracked, tightly closed shells (discard any open ones that do not close when tapped)**

**1 lb 5 oz/600 g thick, boned hake or cod\* fillets, skinned and cut into 2-inch/5-cm chunks**

**12–16 uncooked shrimp, heads and tails removed and deveined (see page 64)**

**thick, crusty bread, to serve**

*\*cook's tips*

Take care not to overcook the hake or it will break into flakes that have very little texture.

Angler fish is an excellent alternative to hake or cod. In fact, vary the ingredients to accommodate whatever firm-fleshed and flaky fish or shellfish are available, but avoid mackerel and salmon, because they are too oily, and swordfish and tuna because their texture is too meaty.

# deep-fried seafood
## *pescadito frito*

*Andalusia is known as the "skillet of Spain," because of the outstanding quality of the deep-fried dishes throughout the region. So, it's no surprise that all along the Mediterranean large and small coastal restaurants feature platters piled high with crisp deep-fried seafood. The fish is always the catch of the day, and few meals can be more enjoyable than sitting under a parasol, sipping a chilled white wine with a selection of deep-fried shrimp and squid rings. You can also use this batter to deep-fry whole baby squid, whitebait, and sardines. Romesco Sauce (see page 233) and Garlic Mayonnaise (see page 232) are both good for dipping the deep-fried fish into.*

1 To make the batter, sift the flour and salt into a bowl and make a well in the center. Slowly add the water and oil, stirring in the liquid until a smooth batter forms; set aside to rest for at least 30 minutes.

2 Pour 3 inches/7.5 cm of oil into a large, heavy-bottom skillet over high heat and heat until it reaches 375°F/190°C, or a cube of day-old bread browns in 30 seconds. Put the seasoned flour in a plastic bag.

3 Place the shrimp in the bag and shake until they are coated with flour. As you remove the shrimp, shake off any excess flour. Drop about 8 shrimp in the skillet, without overcrowding it, and cook for 45 seconds. Turn them over with a large slotted spoon and continue cooking until the shrimp are golden brown and floating on the surface. Use a slotted spoon to transfer them to crumpled paper towels and drain very well. Sprinkle with salt and keep in a warm oven while you cook the remainder.

4 Reheat the oil to the correct temperature between batches and continue deep-frying until all the seafood, including the squid tentacles, is cooked. Garnish with parsley, and serve hot with lemon wedges.

**SERVES 4–6**

*for the batter*

**generous ³/₄ cup self-rising flour**

**¹/₂ tsp salt**

**²/₃ cup water**

**2 tbsp olive oil**

**olive oil, for deep-frying**

**all-purpose flour seasoned with salt and pepper and mild Spanish paprika, to taste**

**24 uncooked large shrimp, shelled and deveined (see page 64)**

**2 large squid, prepared (see page 122), and cut into ¹/₄-inch/5-mm thick rings**

**reserved squid tentacles**

**salt**

**flat-leaf parsley, to garnish**

**lemon wedges, to serve**

# fish baked in salt
## dorada a la sal

When temperatures rise in Palma, Majorca's capital, locals head to the picturesque harbor at Andratx for a relaxed Sunday meal. This dish is a speciality at the numerous small restaurants lining the harbor. The salt-encrusted fish is brought unceremoniously to the table in well-worn, battered roasting pans, where the salt crust is cracked and the moist fish is filleted and served.

Dorada, a member of the bream family, is a popular choice all along the Mediterranean, with a fine texture that makes it favored by cooks. Unfortunately, it is only available in large fish markets away from the Mediterranean, so the best alternative is gilthead bream. (This fish gets its name from the "gold" spot on either side of the head.) When it isn't available, try bream or sea bass.

SERVES 4

2 lb/900 g salt

1 cup all-purpose flour

1 cup water

1 dorada or gilthead bream, about 2¼ lb/1 kg, cleaned
through the gills*

2 lemon slices

few sprigs fresh parsley

1 Preheat the oven to 450°F/230°C. Mix the salt and flour in a bowl and make a well in the center. Pour in the water to make a thick paste; set the mixture aside.

2 Push the lemon and parsley into the gill cavity. Use paper towels to wipe the fish dry. Cover the fish with the salt paste, using your hands. (It's not necessary to scale the fish before you add the paste, but do take care not to cut yourself.) Place in a roasting pan, making sure the fish is completely covered.

3 Roast the fish in the oven for 30 minutes. Remove from the oven and crack the crust. As you pull the crust back, it should bring the skin with it. Fillet the flesh and serve at once.

*cook's tip

Cleaning the fish through the gills keeps it in one piece, retaining both moisture and flavor. A fish merchant will do this for you, but with practice it can be done at home. Push back the flap over the gills and use your fingers to pull them out: be careful because they are sharp. Put your little finger into the cavity and use it to "hook" the innards, then pull them out in one swift movement. Use a teaspoon to scrape out anything left behind. Rinse the fish inside and out under cold water, then pat dry with paper towels.

# salt cod with mashed potatoes
## *brandada*

*Culinary folklore maintains there is a* brandada *recipe for every day of the year. This is a legacy from the days when poor transportation meant salt cod was a dietary staple throughout the winter; as well as on Fridays and during Lent, when the Catholic Church prohibited meat-eating. Although this preparation— with olive oil and mashed potatoes—has its origins in the south of France, it has crossed the border and is well established in Catalonia. Note that the dried salt cod (which you can find in Caribbean as well as Spanish food stores, if it isn't in your supermarket) needs to be soaked for up to 48 hours\*. Pieces of salt cod are not always of a uniform consistency, but select the most even piece available so it will be tender and desalted throughout at the same time.*

### SERVES 4–6

1 lb/450 g dried salt cod, broken into several pieces

4 lemon slices

4 sprigs fresh parsley

2 bay leaves

1 garlic clove, sliced

$^{1}/_{2}$ tsp fennel seeds

$^{1}/_{2}$ tsp black peppercorns, crushed lightly

1 lb 2 oz/500 g fluffy potatoes for mashing,
  peeled and cut into chunks

about 4 tbsp garlic-flavored olive oil

$^{1}/_{2}$ cup milk

lemon juice, to taste

salt and pepper

1 Place the dried salt cod in a large bowl, cover with cold water, and let soak for 48 hours, changing the water at least 3 times a day.

2 When you are ready to cook, put the lemon slices, parsley sprigs, bay leaves, garlic, fennel seeds, and peppercorns in a pan with 5 cups water over high heat and bring to a boil. Reduce the heat and let simmer for 45 minutes.

3 After the salt cod has soaked, transfer it to a large skillet. Add enough of the flavored liquid to cover and bring to a boil. Reduce the heat and let simmer for 45 minutes, or until the fish is tender and flakes easily. Remove the fish from the water. Flake the flesh into fine pieces, removing all skin and tiny bones; set aside.

4 Meanwhile, cook the potatoes in a large pan of boiling salted water until tender; drain well. Put into a large bowl and mash, gradually beating in the flaked salt cod.

5 Put 4 tablespoons of the oil and the milk in a small pan over medium heat and bring them to a simmer. Gradually beat into the salt cod mixture, adding extra until you achieve a consistency you like. Add lemon juice and salt and pepper to taste.

*\*cook's tip*

Not all salt cod is the same, and some pieces can take longer than others to reconstitute and lose the excessive salty flavor. This makes it difficult to give an exact soaking time: it will be at least 24 hours and you should allow up to 48. When the texture loses its hardness, boil a small piece and taste to determine whether it needs to soak for longer.

# hake in white wine
## *merluza a la vasca*

*Spanish cooks are especially fond of using this meaty white-fleshed fish, not least because its mild, nonassertive flavor lends itself to combining with other ingredients. Its cod-like texture means it also can be pan-fried, broiled, baked, and steamed with excellent results.*

*This is a simple and popular dish from the Basque country, but sometimes a more elaborate dish is prepared including clams and shrimp. Asparagus tips, green beans, and peas are other tasty additions.*

**SERVES 4**

**about 2 tbsp all-purpose flour**

**4 hake fillets, about 5 oz/150 g each**

**4 tbsp extra virgin olive oil**

**¹/₂ cup dry white wine, such as a white Rioja**

**2 large garlic cloves, chopped very finely**

**6 scallions, sliced finely**

**2 tbsp fresh parsley, chopped very finely**

**salt and pepper**

1 Preheat the oven to 450°F/230°C. Season the flour generously with salt and pepper on a flat plate. Dredge the skin side of the hake fillets in the seasoned flour, then shake off the excess; set aside.

2 Heat a shallow, flameproof casserole over high heat until you can feel the heat rising. Add the oil and heat until a cube of day-old bread sizzles—it takes about 30 seconds. Add the hake fillets, skin-side down, and cook for 3 minutes until the skin is golden brown.

3 Turn the fish over and season with salt and pepper to taste. Pour in the wine and add the garlic, scallions, and parsley. Transfer the casserole to the preheated oven, uncovered, and bake for 5 minutes, or until the flesh flakes easily. Serve the meal straight from the casserole.

*variation*
When hake isn't available, substitute cod.

# salmon steaks with green sauce
*salmón a la plancha con salsa verde*

*Wild salmon once thrived in northern rivers, but today Spanish cooks, like others throughout Europe, are more likely to buy farmed salmon. This flavor-packed sauce is ideal for perking up the mild taste of the fish, and also works well with broiled beef, veal, pork, and chicken.*

*Sherry Rice (see page 243), Saffron Rice with Green Vegetables (see page 244), or Pan-Fried Potatoes (see page 247) are good accompaniments.*

**SERVES 4**

*for the Green Sauce*

**generous 4 tbsp sprigs fresh flat-leaf parsley**

**8 large fresh basil leaves**

**2 sprigs fresh oregano, or ¹/₂ tsp dried**

**3–4 anchovy fillets in oil, drained and chopped**

**2 tsp capers in brine, rinsed**

**1 shallot, chopped**

**1 large garlic clove**

**2–3 tsp lemon juice, to taste**

**¹/₂ cup extra virgin olive oil**

**4 skinned salmon fillets, each about 5 oz/150 g**

**2 tbsp olive oil**

**salt and pepper**

1 To make the Green Sauce, put the parsley, basil, oregano, anchovies, capers, shallot, garlic, and lemon juice in a food processor or blender and process until chopped. With the motor running, slowly add the oil through the feed tube. Taste and adjust the seasoning, if necessary, remembering that the anchovies and capers can be salty. Pour into a serving bowl, cover with plastic wrap and let chill until required*.

2 When ready to serve, brush the salmon fillets on both sides with the olive oil and season with salt and pepper to taste. Heat a large skillet until you can feel the heat rising from the surface. Add the salmon steaks and cook for 3 minutes. Flip the steaks over and continue cooking for 2–3 minutes until they feel springy and the flesh flakes easily.

3 Serve the hot salmon steaks with a little of the chilled sauce spooned over.

*cook's tip*
The Green Sauce can be prepared up to 2 days in advance and refrigerated until just before serving. The contrast of chilled sauce with hot rich salmon is excellent.

# cod with spinach 169
## *bacalao a la catalana*

*The phrase* a la Catalana *is an indication the dish will contain pine nuts and raisins. In trendy Barcelona restaurants this would be served with broiled tomato halves. It also goes well with Pan-Fried Potatoes (see page 247). A similar dish is made in the Balearic Islands, using Swiss chard rather than spinach.*

**SERVES 4**

*for the Catalan spinach*

¹/₂ **cup raisins**

¹/₃ **cup pine nuts**

**4 tbsp extra virgin olive oil**

**3 garlic cloves, crushed**

**11¹/₄ cups baby spinach leaves, rinsed and shaken dry**

**4 cod fillets, each about 6 oz/175 g**

**olive oil**

**salt and pepper**

**lemon wedges, to serve**

1 Put the raisins for the Catalan spinach in a small bowl, cover with hot water, and set aside to soak for 15 minutes; drain well.

2 Meanwhile, put the pine nuts in a dry skillet over medium-high heat and dry-fry for 1–2 minutes, shaking frequently, until toasted and golden brown: watch closely because they burn quickly.

3 Heat the oil in a large, lidded skillet over medium-high heat. Add the garlic and cook for 2 minutes, or until golden, but not brown. Remove with a slotted spoon and discard.

4 Add the spinach to the oil with only the rinsing water clinging to its leaves. Cover and cook for 4–5 minutes until wilted. Uncover, stir in the drained raisins and pine nuts and continue cooking until all the liquid evaporates. Season to taste and keep warm.

5 To cook the cod, brush the fillets lightly with oil and sprinkle with salt and pepper. Place under a preheated hot broiler about 4 inches/10 cm from the heat and broil for 8–10 minutes until the flesh is opaque and flakes easily.

6 Divide the spinach between 4 plates and place the cod fillets on top. Serve with lemon wedges.

*Spain's food can be as colorful as some of its spectacular works of art*

# flounder for two
## *lenguado para dos*

*In northern Spain, especially round the port of La Coruña, flounder is prized for its tender, delicate flesh, which is suited to this technique of gentle roasting with wine. If flounder isn't available, use sole instead.*

**SERVES 2**

²/₃ **cup olive oil**

**13 oz/375 g waxy potatoes, peeled and sliced thinly**

**1 fennel bulb, trimmed and sliced thinly**

**2 large tomatoes, broiled and peeled, seeded (see page 63), and chopped**

**2 shallots, sliced**

**salt and pepper**

**1 or 2 whole flounder, about 3 lb/1.3 kg, cleaned**

**4 tbsp dry white wine**

**2 tbsp finely chopped fresh parsley**

**lemon wedges, to serve**

1 Spread 4 tablespoons of the oil over the bottom in a shallow roasting pan large enough to hold the flounder. Arrange the potatoes in a single layer, then top with the fennel, tomatoes, and shallots. Season with salt and pepper. Drizzle with an additional 4 tablespoons of the oil. Roast the vegetables in a preheated oven, 400°F/200°C, for 30 minutes.

2 Season the fish with salt and pepper and put on top of the vegetables. Sprinkle with the wine and the remaining 2 tablespoons of oil.

3 Return the roasting pan to the oven and roast the fish, uncovered, for 20 minutes, or until the flesh flakes easily. To serve, skin the fish and remove the fillets. Sprinkle the parsley over the vegetables. Arrange 2–4 fillets on each plate, with the vegetables spooned alongside, and the lemon wedges.

*Water features cool the squares and other public places of many Spanish cities*

# roasted tuna with orange and anchovies    173
## *atún asado con naranja y anchoas*

*Tuna is so abundant in the Strait of Gibraltar and off Spain's southern Atlantic coast that the waters near Cadiz are known as El Mar de Atún, the Tuna Sea. Tuna's rich, meaty flesh makes it ideal for roasting, and in this recipe one thick piece is treated like beef. Serve it with a simple accompaniment, such as Pan-Fried Potatoes (see page 247).*

**SERVES 4–6**

scant 1 cup freshly squeezed orange juice

3 tbsp extra virgin olive oil

2 oz/55 g anchovy fillets in oil, chopped coarsely, with the oil set aside

small pinch dried red pepper flakes, or to taste

pepper

1 tuna fillet, about 20 oz/600 g

1 Combine the orange juice, 2 tablespoons of the olive oil, the anchovies and their oil, the red pepper flakes, and pepper to taste in a nonmetallic bowl large enough to hold the tuna. Add the tuna and spoon the marinade over it. Cover and let chill for at least 2 hours to marinate, turning the tuna occasionally. Remove from the fridge 20 minutes before cooking to bring the fish to room temperature.

2 Remove the tuna from the marinade and wipe dry. Heat the remaining tablespoon of olive oil in a large skillet over high heat. Add the tuna and sear for 1 minute on each side until lightly browned and crisp. Place the tuna in a small roasting pan and cover the pan tightly with foil.

3 Roast in a preheated oven, 425°F/220°C, for 8 minutes for medium-rare and 10 minutes for medium-well done. Remove from the oven and set aside to rest for at least 2 minutes before carving.*

4 Meanwhile, put the marinade in a small pan over high heat and bring to a rolling boil. Boil for at least 2 minutes.

5 Transfer the tuna to a serving platter and carve into thick slices, which will probably break into chunks as you cut them. Serve the sauce separately for spooning over. The tuna can be served hot or at room temperature, but the sauce is best hot.

*cook's tip

Just like beef, roasted tuna continues to cook after it comes out of the oven while it rests. An easy way to check whether the tuna is cooked is to insert a meat thermometer into it, through the foil, just before you put the covered pan in the oven. When the temperature reads 145°F/60°C the tuna will be medium.

# paprika shrimp
*gambas al pimentón*

*Simplicity itself, this recipe captures the flavor of Spanish harborside-eating where the* menú del dia *is determined by the day's catch. Serve these piled on a large platter and let everyone help themselves, breaking off the heads and tails. A glass or two of crisp white wine and plenty of crusty bread are the ideal accompaniments.*

*For a summer lunch these are delicious served with Orange and Fennel Salad (see page 109), or Sherry Rice (see page 243).*

**SERVES 4–6**

**16–24 large, uncooked jumbo shrimp**

**6 tbsp extra virgin olive oil**

**1 large garlic clove, crushed**

**¹/₂ tsp mild paprika, or to taste**

**salt**

**lemon wedges, to serve**

1 Remove the shell from the center of the shrimp, leaving the heads and tails intact. Devein the shrimp (see page 64).

2 Mix together the oil, garlic, paprika, and salt in a shallow dish large enough to hold the shrimp in a single layer. Stir together, then add the shrimp and turn so they are coated. Cover with plastic wrap and let marinate in the fridge for at least 1 hour.

3 When ready to cook, heat a large, ridged cast-iron grill pan over medium-high heat until you can feel the heat rising. Add as many shrimp as will fit without overcrowding the grill pan. Cook about 1 minute until the shrimp curl and the shells turn pink. Turn over and continue cooking for an additional minute, or until cooked through. Drain well on paper towels and keep hot while you continue cooking the remainder.

4 Serve at once with lemon wedges for squeezing over the shrimp.

*variation*

The marinated shrimp are also delicious deep-fried. Remove the heads and devein the shrimp, then marinate as above in step 2. Prepare the batter in the recipe for Pan-Fried Pickled Angler Fish (see page 55). Heat enough olive oil in a large, heavy-bottom pan for deep-frying until a cube of day-old bread sizzles—this takes about 40 seconds. Dip the spicy shrimp in the batter, then deep-fry for 1¹/₂–2 minutes until curled and golden brown. Cook in batches if necessary, to avoid overcrowding the grill pan. Sprinkle the shrimp with coarse sea salt and serve with lemon wedges for squeezing over.

*Eggs, be they baked, scrambled or pan-fried, are always popular in Spain, and often served as a course on their own or as a light meal, such as the late evening meal. A la flamenca refers to the colorful appearance of this popular dish. Vegetarian dishes are few and far between in Spain, but this one is easily adapted by omitting the chorizo.*

1 Heat the oil in a heavy-bottom skillet over medium-high heat. Add the bell peppers and onion and cook for 2 minutes, then add the garlic, chorizo, and paprika, and continue to cook for an additional 3 minutes, or until the bell peppers and onion are soft, but not brown.

2 Stir in the tomatoes with their juices, the sugar, and salt and pepper to taste and bring to a boil. Reduce the heat and let simmer for about 10 minutes, uncovered.

3 Add the potatoes, beans, and peas, and continue simmering for 6–7 minutes until the potatoes are heated through and the beans and peas are cooked.

4 Divide the vegetable mixture between 4 small earthenware casseroles or individual serving dishes and adjust the seasoning if necessary. Crack an egg on top of each. Put in a preheated oven, 350°F/180°C, and bake for 10 minutes, or until the yolks are set as desired. Serve at once.

*cook's tip
Spaniards are exceptionally fond of canned vegetables, and this is one dish in which they are often used. Canned artichoke hearts, asparagus tips, diced carrots or turnips, and peas are all suitable. Drain the vegetables well, then add them at the end of step 2 and skip step 3.

# eggs on vegetables  177
## *huevos a la flamenca*

**SERVES 4**

4 tbsp extra virgin olive oil

2 green bell peppers, cored, seeded, and chopped

1 large onion, chopped

2 garlic cloves, crushed

12 chorizo slices, each about ¹/₄ inch/5 mm thick, casings removed, if preferred

¹/₄ tsp Spanish mild or smoked paprika

1 lb 12 oz/800 g canned chopped tomatoes

pinch of sugar

salt and pepper

8 oz/225 g new potatoes, cooked and chopped into ¹/₂-inch/1-cm cubes*

3¹/₂ oz/100 g green beans, chopped

scant 1 cup frozen or fresh shelled peas

4 large eggs

# broiled bell pepper salad
## *ensalada de pimientos*

*Popular throughout the Mediterranean, this summer salad is ideal for serving on blazing hot days. To make it more substantial, add soaked and boiled salt cod (see page 162).*

**SERVES 4–6**

**6 large red, orange, or yellow bell peppers, each cut in half lengthwise, broiled, and peeled (see page 74)**

**4 hard–cooked eggs, shelled**

**12 anchovy fillets in oil, drained**

**12 large black olives**

**extra virgin olive oil or garlic–flavored olive oil**

**sherry vinegar**

**salt and pepper**

**country–style crusty bread, to serve**

1 Remove any cores and seeds from the broiled bell peppers and cut into thin strips. Arrange on a large serving platter.

2 Cut the eggs into wedges and arrange over the bell pepper strips, along with the anchovy fillets and olives.

3 Drizzle oil over the top, then splash with sherry vinegar, adding both to taste. Sprinkle a little salt and pepper over the top and serve with bread.

*The cable car above Barcelona is a great way to see the city*

# tuna and bean salad
## *ensalada de atún y judías*

**SERVES 4–6**

*for the dressing*

handful of fresh mint leaves, shredded

handful of fresh parsley leaves, chopped

1 garlic clove, crushed

4 tbsp extra virgin olive oil

1 tbsp red wine vinegar

salt and pepper

7 oz/200 g green beans

14 oz/400 g canned small white beans, such as
  cannellini, rinsed and drained

4 scallions, chopped finely

2 fresh tuna steaks, about 8 oz/225 g each and
  $^3/_4$ inch/2 cm thick

olive oil, for brushing

2$^1/_4$ cups cherry tomatoes, halved

salad greens

country-style crusty bread, to serve

mint and parsley leaves, to garnish

1 First, make the dressing. Put all the ingredients, with salt and pepper to taste, into a screw-top jar and shake until blended. Pour into a large bowl and set aside.

2 Bring a pan of lightly salted water to a boil. Add the beans and cook for 3 minutes. Add the white beans and continue cooking for about 4 minutes until the green beans are tender-crisp and the white beans are heated through. Drain well and add to the bowl with the dressing, along with the scallions; toss together.

3 To cook the tuna, heat a ridged grill pan over high heat. Lightly brush the tuna steaks with a little oil on one side, then put oiled side down on the grill pan and cook for 2 minutes. Brush the top side with oil, then turn the steak over and continue cooking for 2 minutes for rare or up to 4 minutes for well done.

4 Remove from the grill pan and let the tuna stand for 2 minutes, or until completely cool. When ready to serve, add the tomatoes to the beans and toss lightly. Line a serving platter with salad greens and pile on the bean salad. Flake the tuna over the top. Serve warm or at room temperature with plenty of bread, garnished with the herbs.

# moors and christians
## *moros y cristianos*

*From Valencia in the Levant, few Spanish dishes can be as directly tied to historical events as this one: the black beans represent the occupying Moors, surrounded by the white rice representing the Christians, who finally triumphed over the Arabs and expelled them from the Iberian Peninsula.*

*Visit small villages in The Levant at the end of April and you will come across Moros y Cristianos festivals, with staged battles—and this dish, to celebrate the victory.*

**SERVES 4–6**

*for the rice*

2 tbsp olive oil

1⁷/₈ cup Spanish short-grain rice, rinsed until the
    water runs clear

4 cups vegetable stock, not from a cube, hot

salt and pepper

*for the beans*

2 tbsp olive oil

2 oz/55 g serrano ham in one piece, diced, or prepared
    lardons

2 large green bell peppers, cored, seeded, and chopped
    finely

1 large onion, chopped finely

2 large garlic cloves, crushed

1 fresh red chile, seeded and chopped finely, or to taste

1 lb 12 oz/800 g canned black beans, drained and rinsed

scant 1¹/₄ cups vegetable stock, not from a cube

2 tbsp sherry vinegar

4 tbsp chopped fresh parsley

1 To make the rice, heat the oil in a shallow, heavy-bottom flameproof casserole. Add the rice and stir until it is coated in oil. Pour in the stock, season to taste, and bring to a boil. Reduce the heat and let simmer for 20 minutes, uncovered and without stirring, until most of the stock is absorbed and small holes appear on the surface. If any liquid remains, cover, remove from the heat, and let stand for 10 minutes.

2 Meanwhile, to make the beans, heat the oil in a large skillet or flameproof casserole. Add the ham and cook for 2 minutes to flavor the oil. Add the bell peppers and onion and cook for 3 minutes, then add the garlic and chile and cook for an additional 2 minutes, or until the onion is softened, but not browned.

3 Stir in the beans and continue cooking for 1–2 minutes. Add the stock and bring to a boil. reduce the heat, and let simmer, uncovered, for about 10 minutes until the stock has evaporated and the bell peppers are very tender. Taste and adjust the seasoning, remembering that the ham can be salty; set aside.

4 Grease the inside of a 6-cup ring mold. Pack the rice into the mold, smoothing the surface*. Reheat in a preheated oven, 300°F/150°C, for about 10 minutes. Reheat the beans, if necessary, then stir in the sherry vinegar and parsley.

5 Using an oven mitt, put a large serving plate face down on top of the ring mold, then invert, giving a sharp shake halfway over. Carefully lift off the mold. Spoon the bean mixture into the center and serve.

*cook's tip*
Both the rice and the bean mixture can be prepared up to a day in advance and chilled overnight in the fridge. Remove the rice mold from the fridge at least 15 minutes before reheating as in step 4.

# DESSERTS

Perhaps the most distinguishable feature of Spanish desserts is how few there are. Everyday meals at home are just as likely to end with fresh, juicy fruit, creamy sheep's cheese, or a pot of yogurt.

With the Moorish occupation of Spain in AD 711 came the introduction of the exotic spices that are still used to flavor Spanish desserts, as well as the cornucopia of fruits—apricots, cherries, citrus fruits, figs, quince, passion fruit, peaches, plums, and dates—that are enjoyed. The generous use of almonds both in desserts and confectionery is also inherited from the style of Arabic cooking. Poached Fruit, Seville Style (see page 215), "Jeweled" Honey Mousses (see page 207), and Dates Stuffed with Spanish Marzipan (see page 225) all reflect the glories of Moorish cuisine.

Yet the golden-topped, orange-flavored Spanish Caramel Custard (see page 192), or *flan*, is universally popular, served both in homes and restaurants. Traditionally it is a baked, rich combination of eggs and milk, but in Valencia, the center of Spain's orange-growing region, orange juice replaces some of the milk.

Another dessert whose popularity has spread through the country is *crema catalana*, Catalonia's version of the French *crème brûlée*—a dish of creamy custard with just a hint of lemon topped with a wafer-thin layer of crisp caramel (see page 195). There must be few people who don't enjoy the taste sensation of the creaminess combined with the slightly burned-tasting caramel. (It is another point of contention with neighboring France, but Spanish food historians maintain that Catalans were enjoying the burned sugar topping for hundreds of years before *crème brûlée* first appeared in any French cookbook.)

Some childhood desserts never fall out of fashion, and you won't find many Spanish adults who will turn down an offer of Deep-Fried Pastries (see page 221) or Pan-Fried Milk (see page 222).

Homemade ice cream is a perennially popular treat. Preserve the fresh flavor of the all-too-quick blood orange season in spring with Blood Orange Ice Cream (see page 204), a perfect dessert for a dinner party. Frozen Almond Cream (see page 201) is easy to make and ideal for anyone who is concerned about eating raw egg yolk, because it doesn't contain any. The hot chocolate sauce that accompanies this recipe is a good all-rounder to add a homemade touch to store-bought ice cream.

Creamy Rice Pudding (see page 196) is a favorite from northern Cantabria. It is a versatile dessert for

*Preserve the fresh flavor of the all-too-quick blood orange season in spring with Blood Orange Ice Cream, a perfect dessert for a dinner party*

any time of year—serve it warm with extra cream for pouring over in winter, or chilled with a fresh fruit salad in the summer.

Lingering over a cup of coffee is a popular Spanish pastime, and Musicians' Bars (see page 224) and Dates Stuffed with Spanish Marzipan (see page 225) are after-dinner candies that will always be appreciated. The Musicians' Bars are slabs of crisp caramel with dried fruit and mixed nuts pressed into it, and they make good hostess gifts to take to dinner parties.

Overleaf *The dry and dusty landscape of Spain's arid heart is home to vines and olives which almost bake in the heat*

# spanish caramel custard
## *flan*

*This is possibly the best-known Spanish dessert outside Spain, which isn't surprising as it is probably the most popular in Spain. You'll find this on menus everywhere, although in Valencia it is often made with orange juice, rather than a custard base. What is common to most tart recipes, however, is the use of extra egg yolks, which give richness (sherry producers once clarified their product with egg whites, so clever cooks developed recipes that made the most of the leftover yolks).*

**SERVES 6**

scant 2¹/₂ cups whole milk

¹/₂ orange with 2 long, thin pieces of rind removed

1 vanilla bean, split, or ¹/₂ tsp vanilla extract

scant 1 cup superfine sugar

butter, for greasing the dish

3 large eggs, plus 2 large egg yolks

1 Pour the milk into a pan with the orange rind and vanilla bean or extract. Bring to a boil, then remove from the heat and stir in ¹/₂ cup of the sugar; set aside for at least 30 minutes to infuse.

2 Meanwhile, put the remaining sugar and 4 tablespoons of water in another pan over medium-high heat. Stir until the sugar dissolves, then boil without stirring until the caramel turns deep golden brown.

3 Immediately remove the pan from the heat and squeeze in a few drops of orange juice to stop the cooking. Pour into a lightly buttered 5-cup soufflé dish and swirl to cover the base; set aside.

4 When the milk has infused, return the pan to the heat, and bring the milk to a simmer. Beat the whole eggs and egg yolks together in a heatproof bowl. Pour the warm milk into the eggs, whisking constantly. Strain this mixture into the soufflé dish.

5 Place the soufflé dish in a roasting pan and pour in enough boiling water to come halfway up the sides of the dish. Bake in a preheated oven, 325°F/160°C, for 75–90 minutes until set and a knife inserted in the center comes out clean.

6 Remove the soufflé dish from the roasting pan and set aside to cool completely. Cover and let chill overnight.

7 To serve, run a metal spatula round the side of the dish, then invert onto a serving plate with a rim, shaking firmly to release.

*San Sebastian is a thriving cultural center and a popular destination for tourists*

# catalan burned cream
## *crema catalana*

*This classic rich, creamy dessert with its "burned"
sugar topping is from Catalonia. Outward
appearances lead one to think this is the same as the
French* crème brûlée, *but the difference lies under the
crisp, caramelized topping. Unlike its French cousin,
this dessert isn't baked, so it remains runny. Prepare
the custard at least 12 hours in advance, to let it
thicken in the fridge.*

### SERVES 6

**3 cups whole milk**

**1 vanilla bean, split**

**thinly pared rind of $\frac{1}{2}$ lemon**

**7 large egg yolks**

**1 cup superfine sugar**

**3 tbsp cornstarch**

*Classical grandeur abounds in Madrid in
the form of carved columns and statues*

1 Prepare the custard a day in advance of serving. Pour
the milk into a pan with the vanilla bean and lemon
rind. Bring to a boil, then remove from the heat and set
aside for at least 30 minutes to infuse.

2 Select a heatproof bowl that will fit over a pan
without touching the bottom. Put the eggs and
$\frac{1}{2}$ cup sugar in the bowl and beat until the sugar
dissolves and the mixture is thick and creamy.

3 Return the infused milk to the heat and bring to a
simmer. Stir 4 tablespoons of the warm milk into a
small bowl with the cornstarch, stirring until a smooth
paste forms. Stir this paste into the simmering milk and
stir over medium-low heat for 1 minute.

4 Strain the milk into the egg mixture and whisk until
well blended. Rinse out the pan and put a small
amount of water in the bottom. Place the pan over
medium-high heat and bring the water to a simmer.
Reduce the heat, put the bowl on top, and stir for
25–30 minutes until the custard is thick enough to coat

the back of the spoon; the water must not touch the
base of the bowl or the eggs might scramble.

5 Divide the mixture between 6 x 4-inch/10-cm
round earthenware serving dishes called *cazuelas*
or flat, white French *crème brûlée* dishes. Let cool
completely, then cover and let chill for at least 12 hours.

6 To serve, sprinkle the top of each with a thin layer
of superfine sugar. In Catalonia, the tops are
caramelized with a special flat iron that is heated in a
gas flame and then placed on top of the sugar. Unless
you happen to have one of these, use a kitchen
blowtorch; a broiler isn't hot enough. Let stand while
the caramel hardens, then serve. The caramel will remain
firm for about 1 hour at room temperature; do not
return to the fridge or the caramel will "melt."

# rice pudding
## *arroz con leche*

Northern Cantabria produces some of Spain's richest dairy products, so it is not surprising that the region's versions of this popular, comforting dessert are made with large quantities of whole milk. This is a thick, creamy dessert that tastes equally good warmed or chilled. It can also be served with light brown sugar sprinkled over the top, or with Poached Fruit, Seville Style (see page 215), or with chopped Caramelized Almonds (see page 96) instead of the sugar.

**SERVES 4–6**

1 large orange

1 lemon

4 cups milk

generous 1 cup Spanish short-grain rice

¹/₂ cup superfine sugar

1 vanilla bean, split

pinch of salt

¹/₂ cup heavy cream

brown sugar, to serve (optional)

1 Finely grate the rinds from the orange and lemon; set aside. Rinse a heavy-bottom pan with cold water and do not dry it.

2 Put the milk and rice in the pan over medium-high heat and bring to a boil. Reduce the heat and stir in the superfine sugar, vanilla bean, orange and lemon rinds, and salt, and let simmer, stirring frequently, until the pudding is thick and creamy and the rice grains are tender: this can take up to 30 minutes, depending on how wide the pan is.

3 Remove the vanilla bean and stir in the cream. Serve at once, sprinkled with brown sugar, if desired, or let cool completely, cover, and let chill until required. (The pudding will thicken as it cools, so stir in extra milk, if necessary.)

*Architecture on such a grand scale is testimony to Spain's rich history*

# rich chocolate cake
## *pastel de chocolate*

*Rich chocolate cakes, such as this, are ideal to enjoy with midmorning coffee or afternoon tea. It's not unusual to see cakes sitting on top of Spanish bars for when customers stop in for a cup of coffee, rather than a beer or sherry.*

*This cake keeps for up to 4 days wrapped in foil.*

**MAKES 10–12 SLICES**

generous ¹/₂ cup raisins

finely grated rind and juice of 1 orange

6 oz/175 g butter, diced, plus extra for greasing the pan

3¹/₂ oz/100 g semisweet chocolate, at least 70% cocoa
  solids, broken up

4 large eggs, beaten

¹/₂ cup superfine sugar

1 tsp vanilla extract

³/₈ cup all-purpose flour

generous ¹/₂ cup ground almonds

¹/₂ tsp baking powder

pinch salt

scant ¹/₂ cup blanched almonds, toasted and chopped

confectioners' sugar, sifted, to decorate

1 Put the raisins in a small bowl, add the orange juice, and let soak for 20 minutes. Line a deep 10-inch/25-cm round cake pan with a removable bottom with waxed paper and grease the paper; set aside.

2 Melt the butter and chocolate together in a small pan over medium heat, stirring. Remove from the heat and set aside to cool.

3 Using an electric mixer beat the eggs, sugar, and vanilla together for about 3 minutes until light and fluffy. Stir in the cooled chocolate mixture.

4 Drain the raisins if they haven't absorbed all the orange juice. Sift over the flour, ground almonds, baking powder, and salt. Add the raisins, orange rind, and almonds, and fold everything together.

5 Spoon into the cake pan and smooth the surface. Bake in a preheated oven, 350°F/180°C, for about 40 minutes, or until a toothpick inserted into the center comes out clean and the cake starts to come away from the side of the pan. Let cool in the pan for 10 minutes, then remove from the pan and let cool completely on a wire rack. Dust the surface with confectioners' sugar before serving.

# frozen almond cream with hot chocolate sauce
## *crema de almendras con salsa de chocolate*

**SERVES 4–6**

**generous 1 cup blanched almonds (see page 50)**

**1¼ cups heavy cream**

**¼ tsp almond extract**

**⅔ cup light cream**

**½ cup confectioners' sugar**

*for the Hot Chocolate Sauce*

**3½ oz/100 g semisweet chocolate, broken into pieces**

**3 tbsp golden syrup**

**4 tbsp water**

**2 tbsp unsalted butter, diced**

**¼ tsp vanilla extract**

1 Place the blanched almonds on a baking sheet and toast in a preheated oven, 400°F/200°C, for 8–10 minutes, stirring occasionally, until golden brown and giving off a "toasted" aroma: watch carefully after 7 minutes because they burn quickly. Immediately pour onto a cutting board and let cool. Coarsely chop scant ½ cup by hand, and finely grind the remainder; set both aside separately.

2 Whip the heavy cream with the almond extract until soft peaks form. Stir in the light cream and continue whipping, sifting in the confectioners' sugar in 3 batches. Transfer to an ice-cream maker and freeze following the manufacturer's instructions*. When the cream is almost frozen, transfer it to a bowl, and stir in the chopped almonds so they are evenly distributed.

3 Put the cream mixture in a 1-lb/450-g loaf pan and smooth the top. Wrap tightly in foil and put in the freezer for at least 3 hours.

4 To make the hot chocolate sauce, place a heatproof bowl over a pan of simmering water. Add the chocolate, syrup, and water and stir until the chocolate melts. Stir in the butter and vanilla extract until smooth.

5 To serve, unwrap the pan and dip the bottom in a sink of boiling water for just a couple of seconds. Invert onto a freezerproof tray, giving a sharp shake until the frozen cream drops out. Using a spatula, coat the top and sides with the finely chopped almonds; return to the freezer unless serving at once.

6 Use a warm knife to slice into 8–12 slices. Arrange 2 slices on each plate and spoon the hot chocolate sauce round.

*\*cook's tips*

If you don't have an ice-cream maker, put the mixture in a freezerproof container and freeze for 2 hours, or until it is starting to thicken and set round the edge. Beat well and return to the freezer until almost frozen. Stir in the almonds and proceed with step 3.

You can make the sauce and the dessert in advance. Remove the dessert from the freezer 15 minutes before serving, and reheat the sauce gently.

# creamy chocolate puddings
## *pudíns de chocolate*

**SERVES 4–6**

6 oz/175 g semisweet chocolate, at least
   70% cocoa solids, broken up

1 1/2 tbsp orange juice

3 tbsp water

2 tbsp unsalted butter, diced

2 eggs, separated

1/8 tsp cream of tartar

3 tbsp superfine sugar

6 tbsp heavy cream

*for the Pistachio-Orange Praline*

corn oil, for greasing

generous 1/4 cup superfine sugar

scant 1/2 cup shelled pistachios

finely grated rind of 1 large orange

1 Melt the chocolate with the orange juice and water in a small pan over very low heat, stirring constantly. Remove from the heat and stir in the butter until melted and incorporated. Using a rubber spatula, scrape the chocolate into a bowl.

2 Beat the egg yolks until blended, then beat them into the chocolate mixture; set aside to cool.

3 In a clean bowl, whisk the egg whites with the cream of tartar until soft peaks form. Gradually beat in the sugar, 1 tablespoon at a time, beating well after each addition, until the meringue is glossy. Beat 1 tablespoon of the meringue mixture into the chocolate mixture, then fold in the rest.

4 In a separate bowl, whip the cream until soft peaks form: do not make it too stiff. Fold into the chocolate mixture. Spoon into individual glass bowls or wine glasses, or 1 large serving bowl. Cover with plastic wrap and let chill for at least 4 hours.

5 Meanwhile, make the praline. Lightly grease a baking sheet with corn oil; set aside. Put the sugar and pistachios in a small pan over medium heat. When the sugar starts to melt, stir gently until a liquid caramel forms and the nuts start popping.

6 Pour the praline onto the baking sheet and immediately finely grate the orange rind over. Let cool until firm. Coarsely chop or finely grind, according to your liking. Cover tightly and store at room temperature until required.

7 Just before serving, sprinkle the praline over the chocolate pudding.

*variations*
Soak the raisins in Spanish brandy or sherry instead of the orange juice. The praline can also be made with blanched almonds or hazelnuts.

# blood orange ice cream
## *helado de naranjas de sangre*

*The Almond Cookies (see page 216) go well with this rich, creamy ice cream.*

**SERVES 4–6**
**3 large blood oranges, washed**
**¹/₃ cup lowfat milk**
**¹/₃ cup light cream**
**generous ⁵/₈ cup superfine sugar**
**4 large egg yolks**
**2 cups heavy cream**
**¹/₈ tsp vanilla extract**

1 Thinly pare the rind from 2 of the oranges, reserving a few strips for decoration, and finely grate the rind from the third. Squeeze the oranges to give ¹/₂ cup juice; set aside.

2 Pour the milk and cream into a pan with the pared orange rind. Bring to a boil, then remove from the heat; set aside for at least 30 minutes to infuse.

3 Select a heatproof bowl that fits over the pan without touching the bottom. Put the sugar and egg yolks in the bowl and beat until thick and creamy.

4 Return the milk mixture to the heat and bring to a simmer. Pour the milk onto the eggs and whisk until well blended. Rinse the pan and put a small amount of water in the bottom. Place over medium heat and bring the water to a simmer. Reduce the heat. Put the bowl on top and stir for about 20 minutes until a thick custard forms that coats the back of the spoon; the water must not touch the bottom of the bowl or the eggs might scramble.

5 Strain the mixture into a clean bowl. Stir in the finely grated orange rind and set aside for 10 minutes.

6 Stir in the reserved juice, heavy cream, and vanilla extract. Transfer to an ice-cream maker and freeze following the manufacturer's instructions. (Alternatively, strain the mixture into a freezerproof container and freeze for 2 hours, or until mushy and freezing round the edges. Tip into a bowl and beat. Return to the freezer and repeat the process twice more.) Remove from the freezer to soften 15 minutes before serving. Decorate with strips of the reserved rind.

*The usual haunts for tourists may not be where to find the best bars and restaurants: follow the locals!*

# lemon sherbet with cava
## *sorbete de limón con cava*

*Once you have frozen the sherbet, this is an almost-instant dinner-party dessert. It will maintain its fresh flavor for up to a month in the freezer.*

**SERVES 4–6**

**3–4 lemons**

**scant 1¼ cups water**

**1 cup superfine sugar**

**1 bottle Spanish cava, chilled, to serve**

1 Roll the lemons on the counter, pressing firmly, which helps to extract as much juice as possible. Pare off a few strips of rind and set aside for decoration, then finely grate the rind from 3 lemons. Squeeze the juice from as many of the lemons as necessary to give ¾ cup.

2 Put the water and sugar in a heavy-bottom pan over medium-high heat and stir to dissolve the sugar. Bring to a boil, without stirring, and boil for 2 minutes. Remove from the heat, stir in the lemon rind, cover, and let stand for 30 minutes, or until cool.

3 When the mixture is cool, stir in the lemon juice. Strain into an ice-cream maker and freeze according to the manufacturer's instructions. (Alternatively, strain the mixture into a freezerproof container and freeze for 2 hours, or until mushy and freezing round the edges. Tip into a bowl and beat. Return to the freezer and repeat the process twice more.) Remove the sherbet from the freezer to soften 10 minutes before serving.

4 To serve, scoop into 4–6 tall glasses, decorate with the reserved rind, if using, and top up with cava.

*variation*
Spaniards also serve lemon sherbet in frozen hollow lemon shells. To do this, slice the tops off 4–6 lemons and use a sharp teaspoon to scoop out the fruit. Spoon the almost-frozen sherbet into the lemons and place in the freezer upright until frozen.

# "jeweled" honey mousses
## *mousse de miel adornado*

**SERVES 6**

1 large egg, plus 3 large egg yolks

¹/₂ cup honey

1¹/₄ cups heavy cream

3 pomegranates, to serve

1 Line 6 ramekins with pieces of plastic wrap large enough to extend over the tops; set aside.

2 Put the whole egg, egg yolks, and honey in a large bowl and beat until blended and fluffy. Put the heavy cream in another bowl and beat until stiff peaks form. Fold the cream into the egg-and-honey mixture.

3 Equally divide the mixture between the ramekins, then fold the excess plastic wrap over the top of each. Place in the freezer for at least 8 hours until firm. These mousses can be served directly from the freezer, because the texture isn't solid.

4 To serve, unfold the plastic wrap, then invert each ramekin onto a serving plate and remove the ramekin and plastic wrap. Cut the pomegranates in half and hold one half over a mousse in turn. Use your other hand to tap firmly on the base of the pomegranate, so the seeds fall over the mousse. Serve at once.

Overleaf *The Moorish influence on architecture is apparent in many Spanish urban landscapes*

# baked apricots with honey
## *albaricoques al horno con miel*

**SERVES 4**

**butter, for greasing**

**4 apricots, each cut in half and pitted**

**4 tbsp slivered almonds**

**4 tbsp honey**

**pinch ground ginger or grated nutmeg**

**vanilla ice cream, to serve (optional)**

1 Lightly butter an ovenproof dish large enough to hold the apricot halves in a single layer.

2 Arrange the apricot halves in the dish, cut sides up. Sprinkle with the almonds and drizzle the honey over. Dust with the spice.

3 Bake in a preheated oven, 400°F/200°C, for 12–15 minutes until the apricots are tender and the almonds golden. Remove from the oven and serve at once, with ice cream on the side, if desired.

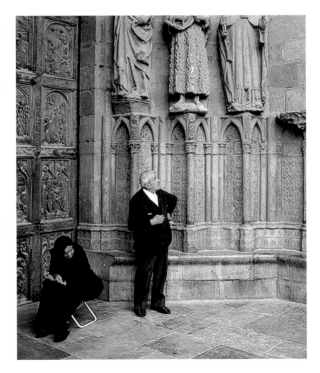

*Few can fail to be overawed by the splendour of church architecture and detailing*

# valencia caramel oranges
## *naranjas de valencia con caramelo*

*Vast orange groves in and round Valencia supply Europe with the juicy fruit. This simple dessert can be prepared up to a day ahead and chilled until required. It is a refreshing end to a meal and delicious served on its own or spooned over vanilla or chocolate ice cream.*

**SERVES 4–6**

**4 large, juicy oranges**

**generous 1¼ cups superfine sugar**

**1¼ cups water**

**4–6 tbsp slivered almonds, toasted, to serve**

1 Working over a heatproof bowl to catch any juices, and using a small serrated knife, pare the oranges, taking care not to leave any of the bitter-tasting pith. Use the knife to remove the orange segments, cutting between the membranes. Squeeze the empty membranes over the bowl to extract as much juice as possible; discard the membranes and set the segments and juice aside.

2 Put the sugar and ⅔ cup of the water into a small, heavy-bottom pan over medium-high heat. Stir until the sugar dissolves, then bring to a boil and boil, without stirring, until the syrup turns a rich golden brown.

3 Pour the remaining water into the pan (stand back because the caramel will splatter). Stir again until the caramel dissolves. Remove from the heat and let the caramel cool slightly, then pour over the oranges. Stir to blend the orange juice into the caramel. Let the oranges cool completely, then cover with plastic wrap and let chill for at least 2 hours before serving.

4 Just before serving, sprinkle the caramel oranges with the toasted slivered almonds.

# poached fruit, seville style
### *frutas escalfadas a la sevillana*

*The Moorish influence on Spanish cuisine is so evident in Andalusia, with the generous use of fruit and spices. Tender, juicy apricots are used in this recipe, but many other tree fruits, such as pears or nectarines, are also delicious. The fruit and syrup can be served on their own, or with vanilla ice cream, Rice Pudding (see page 196) or Deep-Fried Pastries (see page 221).*

**SERVES 4–6**

*for the syrup*

¹/₂ **tsp fennel seeds**

¹/₂ **tsp coriander seeds**

¹/₄ **tsp black peppercorns**

**1 cup superfine sugar**

**1 cup red wine, such as Rioja**

**1 cup water**

**3 tbsp freshly squeezed orange juice**

**2 tbsp freshly squeezed lemon juice**

**2 tbsp Spanish cream sherry**

**3 cloves**

**1 cinnamon stick**

**12 tender apricots, halved and pitted**

**2 tbsp slivered almonds, toasted, to decorate**

1 First, make the red wine syrup. Put the fennel and coriander seeds and peppercorns in a heavy-bottom pan over high heat and dry-fry for up to about 1 minute until they start to give off an aroma. Immediately tip them out of the pan to stop the cooking. Put in a mortar and lightly crush.

2 Put the sugar, wine, water, orange and lemon juices, sherry, and all the spices into a heavy-bottom pan over medium-high heat, stirring to dissolve the sugar. Bring to a boil, without stirring, and let bubble for 5 minutes.

3 Add the fruit and let simmer for 6–8 minutes until tender. Remove the pan from the heat and transfer to a bowl of iced water and let cool. When cool enough to handle, remove the apricots, and peel. Cover and let chill until required.

4 Meanwhile, return the juices to the heat and boil until the syrup thickens and the flavors become more concentrated. Remove from the heat and let cool.

5 When ready to serve, place the fruit in serving bowls, spoon the syrup over, then sprinkle with slivered almonds.

# almond cookies
## *galletas de almendras*

*Rich almond cookies like these are eaten at Easter, and pastry stores will have tempting trays of them on display in their windows.*

**MAKES ABOUT 60**

5$\frac{1}{2}$ oz/150 g butter, at room temperature

generous $\frac{3}{4}$ cup superfine sugar

scant $\frac{7}{8}$ cup all-purpose flour

generous $\frac{1}{4}$ cup ground almonds

pinch of salt

generous $\frac{1}{2}$ cup blanched almonds (see page 50),
   toasted lightly and chopped finely

finely grated rind of 1 large lemon

4 medium egg whites

1 Put the butter and sugar into a bowl and beat until light and fluffy. Sift over the flour, ground almonds, and salt, tipping in any ground almonds left in the strainer. Use a large metal spoon to fold in the chopped almonds and lemon rind.

2 In a separate, spotlessly clean bowl, whisk the egg whites until soft peaks form. Fold the egg whites into the almond mixture.

3 Drop small teaspoonfuls of the cookie mixture onto 1 or more well-greased baking sheets, spacing them well apart. (You might need to cook in batches.) Bake in a preheated oven, 350°F/180°C, for 15–20 minutes until the cookies are golden brown on the edges. Transfer to a wire rack to cool completely. Continue baking until all the mixture is used. Store in an airtight container for up to 1 week.

*Fresh, colorful market produce is daily carried away, somewhere—somehow—in every Spanish town and city*

# almond tart
## *tarta de santiago*

*Almond tarts are not just served for dessert in Spain—chances are you'll find one at any takeout coffee bar, where it will be enjoyed with the endless cups of coffee drunk during the day. The tart's popularity reaches a peak in Santiago de Compostela, home of the cathedral of St James, which thousands of pilgrims visit each year, carrying scallop shells as the symbol of the saint. Silver templates are used to mark the cross of St James on the confectioners' sugar-covered tarts in the city, but an upturned scallop shell makes a good alternative. Position a cleaned scallop shell in the center of the tart and heavily dredge confectioners' sugar over the top. Carefully remove the shell to reveal its impression.*

**MAKES 1 X 10-INCH/25-CM TART**

*for the pie dough*

**2 cups all-purpose flour**

**generous ³/₄ cup superfine sugar**

**1 tsp finely grated lemon rind**

**pinch of salt**

**5¹/₂ oz/150 g unsalted butter, chilled and cut into small dice**

**1 medium egg, beaten lightly**

**1 tbsp chilled water**

**6 oz/175 g unsalted butter, at room temperature**

**scant ⁷/₈ cup superfine sugar**

**3 large eggs**

**generous 1¹/₂ cups finely ground almonds**

**2 tsp all-purpose flour**

**1 tbsp finely grated orange rind**

**¹/₂ tsp almond extract**

**confectioners' sugar, to decorate**

**sour cream (optional), to serve**

**1** First, make the pie dough. Put the flour, sugar, lemon rind, and salt in a bowl. Rub or cut in the butter until the mixture resembles fine bread crumbs. Combine the egg and water, then slowly pour into the flour, stirring with a fork until a coarse mass forms. Shape into a ball and let chill for at least 1 hour.

**2** Roll out the pie dough on a lightly floured counter* until ¹/₈ inch/3 mm thick. Use to line a greased 10-inch/25-cm tart pan with a removable bottom. Return the tart pan to the fridge for at least 15 minutes.

**3** Cover the pastry shell with foil and fill the tart with pie weights or dried beans. Place in a preheated oven, 425°F/220°C, and bake for 12 minutes. Remove the pie weights and foil and return the pastry shell to the oven for 4 minutes to dry the base. Remove from the oven and reduce the oven temperature to 400°F/200°C.

**4** Meanwhile, make the filling. Beat the butter and sugar until creamy. Beat in the eggs, 1 at a time. Add the almonds, flour, orange rind, and almond extract, and beat until blended.

**5** Spoon the filling into the pastry shell and smooth the surface. Bake for 30–35 minutes until the top is golden and the tip of a knife inserted in the center comes out clean. Let cool completely on a wire rack, then dust with sifted confectioners' sugar (see introduction). Serve with a spoonful of sour cream, if desired.

*cook's tip*
If you have difficulty rolling out this rich pie dough, roll it between two sheets of plastic wrap. Pull off the top sheet, invert the pie dough into the pan and peel off the second sheet. Alternatively, roll out the dough in small pieces and "patch" them together with floured fingers.

# deep-fried pastries
*pasteles fritos*

*A treat for children of all ages!*

**MAKES 16–20**

scant ³/₄ **cup all-purpose flour**

**3 tbsp unsalted butter, melted**

**1 tbsp Spanish cream sherry**

¹/₂ **tsp vanilla extract**

**pinch of salt**

**1 small egg, beaten very lightly**

**olive oil, for deep-frying**

*to decorate*

**2 tbsp confectioners' sugar**

¹/₂ **tsp ground cinnamon**

**pinch of ground ginger**

1 Put the flour in a bowl and make a well in the center. Add the butter, cream sherry, vanilla extract, salt, and 1 tablespoon of the egg, and mix together until a dough forms. Knead the dough in the bowl until it is smooth. Shape into a ball and wrap in plastic wrap; set aside at room temperature for 15 minutes.

2 On a lightly floured counter roll out half the dough very thinly. Use a 2¹/₄-inch/5.5-cm fluted cookie cutter to cut out 8–10 circles, re-rolling the trimmings. Repeat with the remaining dough.

3 Heat 2 inches/5 cm oil in a heavy-bottom skillet over high heat to 350°F/180°C or until a cube of day-old bread turns brown in 35 seconds. Add 5–6 dough circles, without overcrowding the skillet and deep-fry for 45 seconds, turn them over with a large slotted spoon, and continue cooking until the circles are puffed on both sides and golden brown. Transfer to crumpled paper towels and drain very well. Take care: they are delicate and can break easily. Repeat with the remaining dough circles.

4 While the pastries are hot, mix the confectioners' sugar, cinnamon, and ginger together. Use a fine strainer and sift the mixture over the warm pastries. These will keep in an airtight container for up to 3 days.

# pan-fried milk
*leche frita*

**MAKES ABOUT 25**

**peanut or other flavorless oil**

**2¹/₂ cups whole milk**

**1 cinnamon stick**

**1 strip of lemon rind, without any white pith**

**2 large eggs plus 1 large egg yolk**

**¹/₂ cup superfine sugar**

**³/₈ cup all-purpose flour, plus extra for dusting**

**scant ¹/₄ cup cornstarch**

**1 tsp vanilla extract**

**olive oil**

**extra superfine sugar and cinnamon, to decorate**

1 Line a 12 x 9-inch/30 x 23-cm shallow cake pan with foil and lightly grease with the oil; set aside.

2 Pour the milk into a pan with the cinnamon stick and lemon rind. Bring to a boil, then remove from the heat; set aside for at least 30 minutes to infuse.

3 Put the eggs, egg yolk, sugar, flour, cornstarch, and vanilla extract in the bowl and beat until smooth.

4 Return the milk mixture to the heat and bring to a simmer. Pour the milk onto the egg mixture and whisk until well blended. Bring to a boil, stirring, then reduce the heat and let simmer for 2–3 minutes until the custard thickens and leaves the side of the pan.

5 Pour the custard into the prepared shallow pan and use a wet spatula to smooth the surface. Let cool completely, then cover and let chill for 2–3 hours.

6 Invert the custard onto a cutting board and peel off the foil. Cut on the diagonal to make 25 triangles, plus odd pieces of trimming from the edges. Dust the custard triangles in flour and shake off any excess.

7 Heat 2 inches/5 cm of oil in a heavy-bottom sauté pan or skillet over high heat to 350°F/180°C, or until a cube of day-old bread browns in 35 seconds. Add 5–6 custard triangles at a time, without overcrowding the skillet, and cook for 45 seconds. Turn them over with a spatula or slotted spoon; continue cooking until golden brown. Transfer to crumpled paper towels and drain well. Repeat in batches with the remaining triangles. Serve sprinkled with the extra sugar and cinnamon.

*Urban Spaniards retain their love of regional cuisine and top-quality ingredients, despite their modern lifestyle*

# musicians' bars
## *de musico*

These brittle fruit-and-nut bars take their name from the time when troupes of musicians traveled through Spain, performing for festivals and weddings or giving impromptu concerts. Their meager wages might have been a meal, a bed for the night, or whatever dried fruit and nuts were available to provide sustenance on the following day's travels. Today, the culinary legacy is that any tarts or caramel slabs with a mixed fruit-and-nut topping are known as de musico, or musicians' desserts.

**MAKES 3 BARS; EACH BAR SERVES 4–6**

generous 2$\frac{1}{2}$ cups superfine sugar

$\frac{2}{3}$ cup water

$\frac{1}{8}$ tsp white wine vinegar

peanut or other flavorless oil, for greasing

generous 2 cups mixed nuts, such as blanched or unblanched almonds, slivered almonds, skinned hazelnuts, salted or unsalted skinned peanuts, and salted or unsalted pecans

generous $\frac{1}{2}$ cup raisins

generous $\frac{1}{2}$ cup ready-to-eat dried apricots, figs, or dates, chopped very finely

$\frac{1}{2}$ cup pine nuts

1 Put the sugar, water, and vinegar in a heavy-bottom pan over medium-high heat, stirring to dissolve the sugar. Bring to a boil, then boil, without stirring, for 20–25 minutes until the caramel reaches 350°F/175°C on a sugar thermometer, or turns a rich amber color.

2 Meanwhile, generously grease a 12 x 9-inch/ 30 x 23-cm baking pan, and a large chef's knife with the oil; set both aside. Combine the nuts and fruit in a bowl.

3 When the caramel is amber colored, stir in the fruit and nuts, and immediately pour into the prepared baking pan. Work very quickly, using a wet spatula to spread the mixture evenly.

4 Let the caramel stand for a few minutes to set until firm but not too brittle to cut. Invert the caramel bar onto a sheet of greased waxed paper and use the oiled knife to cut into 3 slabs each measuring 4 x 9 inches/10 x 23 cm. Let cool until brittle, then wrap each in foil and store for up to 1 week.

# dates stuffed with spanish marzipan
## *dátiles rellenos de melindres*

*Elche, near Alicante on the Costa Blanca, has had glorious date palms for the past 3,000 years, so it's no surprise that dates are teamed with marzipan, reflecting the Moorish contribution to Spanish food. Spanish marzipan differs from that made in northern Europe as it contains no egg white. The possible flavorings are almost endless: try finely grated orange or lemon rind, very finely chopped candied fruit, or add finely chopped pistachios.*

**MAKES 12–14**

*for the Spanish Marzipan*

⁵/₈ **cup confectioners' sugar, plus extra for dusting**

**generous** ⁵/₈ **cup ground almonds**

¹/₄ **tsp almond extract**

**12–14 ready-to-eat dates**

1 To make the Spanish marzipan, sift the confectioners' sugar then mix with the ground almonds in a bowl. Sprinkle over the almond extract. Gradually add a little water, ¹/₄ teaspoon at a time, until the mixture comes together and can be pressed into a ball.

2 Knead the marzipan in your hands and then on a counter dusted with confectioners' sugar until it is smooth. It is now ready to be used, or can be wrapped in plastic wrap and stored in the fridge for up to 3 days.

3 To stuff the dates, use a small knife to slice along the length of each, then open out and pull out the pit. Break off a small piece of the marzipan and mold it into a "log," pressing it into the date. Arrange the dates on plate and serve with coffee after dinner.

# ACCOMPANIMENTS
# & DRINKS

# Simplicity is one of the hallmarks of Spanish meals, and complicated sauces do not feature widely.

In Catalonia, Romesco Sauce (see page 233), with toasted almonds, tomatoes and hot, sweet dried chiles, has been transformed from being the base of a mixed seafood stew from the coastal town of Tarragona to a sauce that can be served with broiled or baked seafood. (It also livens up a roast chicken and broiled pork chops, even if this pairing is somewhat unconventional.)

In the Canary Islands the sauce to accompany the tapas "Wrinkled" Potatoes (see page 84) is *mojo rojo*, a bright red sauce, traditionally made with hot Spanish paprika and *pimientos del piquillo*. It is just as good with meatballs (see page 77). A green version, *mojo verde*, is flavored with cilantro.

The piquant garlic-flavored mayonnaise, *Allioli*, on the other hand, has a long history, and Spanish food historians claim that it is the forerunner of French mayonnaise. The name literally means "garlic and oil." Its pungency depends on how many garlic cloves are used, and that is a matter of personal taste. Today's version is almost indistinguishable from the *aïoli* of Provençal France, but originally the Spanish sauce consisted simply of crushed garlic with olive oil beaten in drop by drop to form an emulsion. Unfortunately, that technique is quite difficult to master, so egg yolks are almost always included in the modern version, resulting in a thicker, more stable sauce.

*Allioli* is quick and easy to make at home (see page 232), but few Spanish cooks bother because their supermarkets stock numerous brands. (Whenever you do make your own, however, make sure that you store it in the fridge in a covered container and use within 3 days.)

The Pan-Fried Potatoes recipe (see page 247) combines the Spaniards' passion for sautéd foods with their love of potatoes, which appear in various guises in the different regions. These potatoes are a typically Spanish accompaniment to any broiled meat, seafood, or poultry dishes.

Rice, like vegetables, is rarely served as a side-dish accompaniment in Spain, but several recipes are included in this chapter to help with meal planning in other countries. Artichoke Hearts and Peas (see page 248) is almost a meal in itself. Sherry Rice (see page 243) is a sophisticated side dish that complements a roast joint of veal or pork, as well as

*When temperatures are soaring, try icy cold Lemon Water. Its slightly bitter flavor is more refreshing than sweet lemonade.*

Veal with Pickled Vegetables (see page 139). The recipe for Saffron Rice with Green Vegetables (see page 244) is ideal for turning even the simplest broiled lamb chop into a meal.

When temperatures are soaring, try icy cold Lemon Water (see page 252). Its slightly bitter flavor is more refreshing than sweet lemonade. And the classic Sangria (see page 253), the country's favorite choice for summer quaffing, is the perfect way to enjoy the full red wines of Spain and its sun-ripened fruits, combined in a long cool glass.

# garlic mayonnaise
## *allioli*

*One of the classic sauces of Catalan cuisine. This is often served with deep-fried seafood and tapas as a dip, but it is also excellent with simply cooked young vegetables in the spring. (Cook young, tender asparagus, baby carrots, and new potatoes in individual pans of lightly salted boiling water until just tender-crisp. Drain and refresh with ice water to stop overcooking, then pat dry. Arrange a selection on each plate and season with salt and pepper, then add a spoonful of Allioli on the side.)*

*Originally this Spanish sauce was distinctly different from French aïoli because it didn't include egg yolks. The authentic sauce, however, was difficult to make, so today there really isn't any difference between the two versions of garlic mayonnaise.*

**MAKES ABOUT 1½ CUPS**

3–4 large garlic cloves, or to taste

sea salt

2 large egg yolks

1 tsp lemon juice

1¼ cups extra virgin olive oil

salt and pepper

1 Mash the garlic cloves to a paste with a pinch of sea salt. Put the paste in a food processor, add the egg yolks, and lemon juice, and process.

2 With the motor still running, slowly dribble in the olive oil through the feed tube until an emulsion forms and the sauce thickens. Taste and adjust the seasoning. Cover and let chill for up to 3 days.

*variation—Garlic Saffron Sauce*
Soak a large pinch of saffron in 2 tablespoons of hot water for at least 10 minutes. Follow the recipe, and add the saffron water after the sauce thickens in step 2.

# romesco sauce
## romesco

*This Catalan tomato sauce is traditionally served with fish and shellfish, but it is also ideal for adding an instant Spanish flavor to simply cooked chicken, pork, or lamb. Authentic recipes are made with dried romesco chiles, which have a sweet and hot flavor. Unfortunately, they are difficult to obtain outside the region, so this recipe uses a dried ñora chile, which is another sweet variety, with dried hot chiles for the heat.*

**MAKES ABOUT 1¼ CUPS**

4 large, ripe tomatoes

16 blanched almonds (see page 50)

3 large garlic cloves, unpeeled and left whole

1 dried sweet chile, such as ñora, soaked for
   20 minutes and patted dry

4 dried red chiles, soaked for 20 minutes and
   patted dry

pinch of sugar

²/₃ cup extra virgin olive oil

about 2 tbsp red wine vinegar

salt and pepper

1 Place the tomatoes, almonds, and garlic on a baking sheet and roast in a preheated oven, 350°F/180°C, for 20 minutes, but check the almonds after about 7 minutes, because they can burn quickly; remove as soon as they are golden and giving off an aroma.

2 Peel the roasted garlic and tomatoes. Put the almonds, garlic, sweet chile, and dried red chiles in a food processor and process until finely chopped. Add the tomatoes and sugar and process again.

3 With the motor running, slowly add the olive oil through the feed tube. Add 1½ tablespoons of the vinegar and quickly process. Taste and add extra vinegar, if desired, and salt and pepper to taste.

4 Let stand for at least 2 hours, then serve at room temperature. Alternatively, cover and let chill for up to 3 days, then bring to room temperature before serving. Stir in any oil that separates before serving.

# mixed vegetable stew

## *pisto*

*Like ratatouille from neighboring France, this stew is best in the height of summer when vegetable gardens are at their most bountiful. Spaniards often serve this chilled, when it makes a flavorsome salad or tapas spooned onto thick bread slices. Served hot, it makes an ideal accompaniment to broiled chicken breasts or steaks.*

*This version cooks vegetables individually so the flavors remain distinctive.*

**SERVES 4–6**

about ¹/₂ cup olive oil

2 large onions, sliced thinly

4 large garlic cloves, crushed

10 oz/300 g eggplant, cut into ¹/₂-inch/1-cm cubes

10 oz/300 g yellow or green zucchinis, cut into
    ¹/₂-inch/1-cm cubes

1 large red bell pepper, cored, seeded, and chopped

1 large yellow bell pepper, cored, seeded, and chopped

1 large green bell pepper, cored, seeded, and chopped

2 sprigs fresh thyme

1 bay leaf

1 small sprig young rosemary

generous ¹/₃ cup vegetable stock

salt and pepper

1 lb/450 g large, juicy tomatoes, peeled (see page 63),
    seeded, and chopped

1 Heat about 2 tablespoons of the oil in a large, flameproof casserole over medium heat. Add the onions and cook, stirring occasionally, about 5 minutes until they start to soften, but not brown. Add the garlic and stir round. Reduce the heat to very low.

2 Meanwhile, heat a skillet over high heat until you can feel the heat rising. Add 1 tablespoon of the oil and the eggplant cubes to make a single layer. Cook, stirring, until they are slightly brown on all sides. Add to the casserole with the onions.

3 Add another tablespoon of oil to the skillet. Add the zucchinis and cook, stirring, until lightly browned all over. Add the zucchinis to the casserole. Cook the bell peppers the same way, then add to the casserole.

4 Stir the thyme, bay leaf, rosemary, stock, and salt and pepper to taste into the casserole and bring to a boil. Reduce the heat to very low again, cover, and let simmer, stirring occasionally, for about 20 minutes until the vegetables are very tender and blended.

5 Remove the casserole from the heat and stir in the tomatoes. Cover and set aside for 10 minutes for the tomatoes to soften. The *pisto* is now ready to serve, but it is even better if it is left to cool completely and then served chilled the next day.

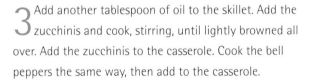

# tomato and bell pepper sauce
*salsa de tomates y pimientos*

*The amount of orange rind you add to this simple, all-purpose sauce really changes its character. Large strips of rind, for example, "lift" the flavors in winter when fresh tomatoes are insipid.*

**MAKES ABOUT 3 CUPS**

4 tbsp olive oil

10 large garlic cloves

5 oz/140 g shallots, chopped

4 large red bell peppers, cored, seeded, and chopped

2 lb 4 oz/1 kg good-flavored ripe, fresh tomatoes, chopped, or 2 lb 12 oz/1.2 kg good-quality canned chopped tomatoes

2 thin strips freshly pared orange rind

pinch hot red pepper flakes (optional), to taste

salt and pepper

1 Heat the olive oil in a large, flameproof casserole over medium heat. Add the garlic, shallots, and bell peppers and cook for 10 minutes, stirring occasionally, until the bell peppers are soft, but not brown.

2 Add the tomatoes, including the juices if using canned ones, orange rind, hot pepper flakes, if using, and salt and pepper to taste and bring to a boil. Reduce the heat to as low as possible and let simmer, uncovered, for 45 minutes, or until the liquid evaporates and the sauce thickens.

3 Purée the sauce through a mouli. Alternatively, purée in a food processor, then use a wooden spoon to press through a fine strainer. Taste and adjust the seasoning if necessary. Use at once, or cover and let chill for up to 3 days.

*Monteagudo in the province of Murcia, where irrigated soils yield vast quantities of rice, vegetables, and fruit for the Spanish table*

# spinach with chickpeas 239
## *espinacas con garbanzos*

*Chickpeas have featured in Andalusian recipes for centuries, and Spanish conquistadors took this rich, nutty legume with them on their long voyages of discovery to the New World. The use of cumin, cayenne, and turmeric in this recipe reflects the North African and Moorish influences on Spanish cuisine. Serve this with any roast or broiled meat, or on its own as a vegetarian dish.*

**SERVES 4–6**

2 tbsp olive oil

1 large garlic clove, cut in half

1 medium onion, chopped finely

¹/₂ tsp cumin

pinch cayenne pepper

pinch turmeric

1 lb 12 oz/800 g canned chickpeas, drained and rinsed

11¹/₄ cups baby spinach leaves, rinsed and shaken dry

2 pimientos del piquillo (see page 67), drained and sliced

salt and pepper

1 Heat the oil in a large, lidded skillet over medium-high heat. Add the garlic and cook for 2 minutes, or until golden, but not brown. Remove with a slotted spoon and discard.

2 Add the onion and cumin, cayenne and turmeric and cook, stirring, about 5 minutes until soft. Add the chickpeas and stir round until they are lightly colored with the turmeric and cayenne.

3 Stir in the spinach with just the water clinging to its leaves. Cover and cook for 4–5 minutes until wilted. Uncover, stir in the *pimientos del piquillo* and continue cooking, stirring gently, until all the liquid evaporates. Season to taste and serve.

Overleaf *An outdoor market offers not only a wide selection of fresh fruit and vegetables, but also the perfect opportunity to study local culture and customs*

# sherry rice
*arroz al jerez*

*An excellent dish to accompany roast veal, pork, or chicken.*

**SERVES 4–6**

2 tbsp olive oil

1 large onion, chopped finely

1 large garlic clove, crushed

$1^7/_8$ cups Spanish short-grain rice

1 cup amontillado sherry

4 cups fresh chicken stock, hot*

pinch of cayenne pepper

salt and pepper

1 Heat the oil in a shallow, heavy-bottom flameproof casserole. Add the onion and cook for 3 minutes, then add the garlic and cook for an additional 2 minutes, or until the onion is soft, but not brown.

2 Rinse the rice until the water runs clear. Drain, then add to the casserole and stir until it is coated in the oil. Add all but 2 tablespoons of the sherry and let it bubble. Pour in the stock with the cayenne and salt and pepper to taste and bring to a boil. Reduce the heat and let simmer for 20 minutes, uncovered and without stirring, until most of the stock is absorbed and small holes appear on the surface.

3 Turn off the heat under the rice, sprinkle with the remaining sherry, cover, and let stand for 10 minutes until all the liquid is absorbed.

*variation—Saffron Sherry Rice*

Bring the stock to a boil in a small pan, add a pinch of saffron threads, and set aside for at least 10 minutes to infuse. Follow the recipe above and use the saffron-flavored stock in step 2.

*\*cook's tip*

It is important not to use stock made from a cube, which tends to be salty and which would mask the delicate flavor of this dish.

*Castles in the air tell of Spain's glorious past*

# saffron rice with green vegetables
*arroz azafranado con verduras*

SERVES 4–6

large pinch saffron threads

5 cups vegetable stock, hot

2 tbsp extra virgin olive oil

1 large onion, chopped finely

1 large garlic clove, crushed

1$^{7}/_{8}$ cup short-grain Spanish rice

3$^{1}/_{2}$ oz/100 g thin green beans, chopped

salt and pepper

scant 1 cup frozen peas

flat-leaf parsley, to garnish

*The sights of Madrid are as exciting and colorful by night as by day*

1 Put the saffron threads in a heatproof bowl and add the hot vegetable stock; set aside to infuse.

2 Meanwhile, heat the oil in a shallow, heavy-bottom flameproof casserole over medium-high heat. Add the onion and cook for about 3 minutes, then add the garlic and cook for an additional 2 minutes, or until the onion is soft, but not brown.

3 Rinse the rice until the water runs clear. Drain, then add with the beans and stir until they are coated with oil. Pour in the stock with salt and pepper to taste and bring to a boil. Reduce the heat and let simmer for 12 minutes, uncovered, and without stirring.

4 Gently stir in the peas and continue simmering for 8 minutes until the liquid has been absorbed and the beans and peas are tender. Taste and adjust the seasoning. Garnish with the parsley and serve.

# pan-fried potatoes 247
## *fritas*

*A popular Spanish way to prepare potatoes, one which is often served with meat or poultry, or as Feisty Potatoes (see page 86).*

**SERVES 6**

**2 lb 4 oz/1 kg potatoes, unpeeled**

**olive oil**

**sea salt**

1 Scrub the potatoes, pat them dry, and cut into chunky pieces.

2 Put ½ inch/1 cm olive oil and 1 potato piece in 1 of 2 large, heavy-bottom skillets over medium-high heat and heat until the potato starts to sizzle. Add the remaining potatoes, without crowding the skillets, and cook for about 15 minutes until golden brown all over and tender. Work in batches, if necessary, keeping the cooked potatoes warm while you cook the remainder.

3 Use a slotted spoon to transfer the potatoes to a plate covered with crumpled paper towels. Blot off any excess oil and sprinkle with sea salt. Serve at once.

*variation—Pan-Fried Garlic Potatoes*
Thinly slice 6 large garlic cloves. Add to the skillet with the potatoes, but only cook until they turn brown. Remove with a slotted spoon: if they burn, the oil will taste burned. Alternatively, cook the potatoes in garlic-flavored olive oil.

*A rampant lion assumes pride of place among the monuments in Madrid*

# artichoke hearts and peas
## *alcachofas y guisantes*

*An ideal accompaniment to roast poultry, but delicious enough to become a light lunch in itself.*

SERVES 4–6

4 tbsp extra virgin olive oil

2 onions, sliced finely

1 large garlic clove, crushed

10 oz/280 g artichoke hearts preserved in oil, drained
   and halved

1³/₄ cups frozen or fresh shelled peas

2 red bell peppers, broiled, seeded (see page 74), and
   sliced

2 thin slices serrano ham, chopped (optional), or
   prosciutto

6 tbsp finely chopped fresh parsley

juice ¹/₂ lemon

salt and pepper

1 Heat the oil in a flameproof casserole over medium-high heat. Add the onions and cook, stirring, for 3 minutes, then add the garlic and cook for 2 minutes until the onions are soft, but not brown.

2 Add the halved artichoke hearts and fresh peas, if using, along with just enough water to cover. Bring to a boil, then reduce the heat and let simmer for 5 minutes, uncovered, or until the peas are cooked through and all the water has evaporated.

3 Stir in the bell peppers, ham, and frozen peas, if using. Continue simmering just long enough to warm through. Stir in the parsley and lemon juice to taste. Add salt and pepper, remembering that the ham is salty. Serve at once, or let cool to room temperature.

*Beautifully designed fountains are among the many splendors of Madrid*

# hot chocolate
## *chocolate*

1 Melt the chocolate in the milk in a heavy-bottom pan over medium heat, stirring constantly. Add the sugar and continue stirring until it dissolves.

2 Put the cornstarch in a small bowl and make a well in the center. Add about 2 tablespoons of the hot liquid and gradually stir the cornstarch into the liquid until a thick, smooth paste forms. Stir in another 2 tablespoons of hot liquid.

3 Stir all the cornstarch mixture into the pan and bring to a simmer, stirring. Bring to a boil and continue stirring until the chocolate thickens. Pour into coffee cups and serve.

*Spaniards love their hot chocolate so thick that it has a coating consistency and you almost need to eat it with a spoon—ideal for dipping in* churros, *Deep-Fried Pastries (see page 221), a great breakfast treat. A small amount of this drink goes a long way because it is so rich.*

### SERVES 4–6
3¹/₂ oz/100 g semisweet chocolate, with at least 70% cocoa, broken up

2¹/₂ cups milk

generous ¹/₂ cup superfine sugar

3¹/₂ tbsp cornstarch

1 tsp vanilla extract

pinch salt

*The sight of a bell tower announces a settlement to the traveler on this steep track*

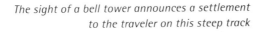

# lemon water
## *agua limón*

**MAKES 4–6 GLASSES**

8 large lemons

1 cup superfine sugar, plus extra to taste

3 cups boiling water

1 Finely grate the rind and squeeze the juice of 7 of the lemons into a large heatproof bowl; remove all the seeds. Finely slice the remaining lemon and set aside 4–6 slices to use for serving; stir the remainder into the juice.

2 Stir the superfine sugar into the bowl. Add the boiling water and let cool to room temperature. Let chill until required.

3 To serve, strain into a serving pitcher and dilute with cold water to taste. Stir in extra sugar, if desired. Serve in chilled glasses, garnishing each one with a slice of lemon.

# sangria

*sangría*

**MAKES 12–15 GLASSES**

generous ¹/₃ cup Spanish brandy

4 large lemons, sliced and quartered

4 large oranges, sliced and quartered

2 limes, sliced and quartered

2 peaches, pitted and sliced (optional)

2 x 75-cl bottles full-flavored Spanish red wine, chilled

1 cup superfine sugar, plus extra to taste

ice cubes, to serve

1 Put the brandy and half the citrus fruit and peach slices, if using, in a bowl and use a wooden spoon to crush the fruit into the brandy. Cover and let chill for at least 2 hours. Cover the remaining fruit slices and let chill until required.

2 Pour the brandy and fruit into a large pitcher, add the wine and the sugar, stirring until dissolved. Taste and add extra sugar, if desired. Place a mixture of the reserved fruit slices in glasses and pour over the Sangria, including some of the brandy-soaked fruit.